The Troller Yacht Book

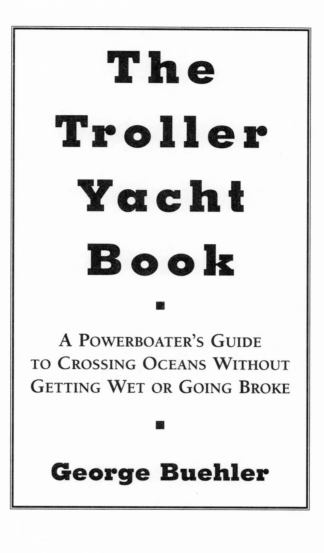

The Troller Yacht Book

A POWERBOATER'S GUIDE
TO CROSSING OCEANS WITHOUT
GETTING WET OR GOING BROKE

George Buehler

W. W. Norton & Company

New York • London

For information about permission to reproduce selections from this book,
write to Permissions, W. W. Norton & Company, Inc., 500 Fifth Avenue,
New York, NY 10110

The text of this book is composed in Berkeley with the display set in Memphis.
Composition by Woody Sherman. Manufacturing by Haddon Craftsmen.
Book design by Pamela Fogg.

Library of Congress Cataloging-in-Publication Data
Buehler, George, 1948-
    The troller yacht book: a powerboater's guide to crossing oceans
    without getting wet or going broke / George Buehler.
        p. cm.
    Includes bibliographical references and index.

    ISBN 0-393-04709-1

    1. Yachts—Design and construction. 2. Motorboats—Design and
    construction. I. Title.
VM331.B848 1999
623.8'231—dc21   98-48052 CIP

W. W. Norton & Company, Inc., 500 Fifth Avenue, New York, NY 10110
http://www.wwnorton.com

W. W. Norton & Company Ltd., 10 Coptic Street, London WC1A 1PU

1 2 3 4 5 6 7 8 9 0

"Oh Lord, please forgive me. I went for a ride on a powerboat, and I LIKED it."

—Anonymous sailor's lament

Contents

Acknowledgments

NO BOOK COMES OUT OF A VACUUM, and this one couldn't have happened without my good luck in living through fascinating times and an extraordinary variety of experiences. And most important, I've known, or sometimes just met briefly, a slew of great people who, in the words of Waylon Jennings, were nice to me.

Fishermen and cruising sailors. Boatbuilders as far apart as Maine and Oregon and Turkey and Brazil. Roustabout characters scattered all over the world doing and talking stuff that got my imagination going. Magazine editors who over the years bought my articles or more often didn't buy them but corresponded with me, sending me down the road of uncertainty, financial insecurity, and great fun.

And no book is solely the result of its author's labors. There is a cover designer and a copy editor and a proofreader and other talented folk who work on it too. And there is always an editor in the background, and I require more of that sort of help than many. This book's editor, Jim Babb, and I worked together on an earlier book, *Buehler's Backyard Boatbuilding*. It came out pretty nicely and, I hear, is still selling. Jim's Southern Cracker Redneck background blends well with my Northwest Pinko Redneck background. And while he tends to cut my more profound observations, calling them ramblings that I've said twice before, he occasionally has a point. His editing skills probably didn't hurt.

And a thanks to John Barstow at W. W. Norton. It's an honor to have the publisher of Howard Chapelle publish my book. Especially since years back, they rejected my boatbuilding book. But that's just payin' the dues, and I'm pleased and grateful that they have published *The Troller Yacht Book*.

Ocean Cruising in Powerboats?

WHEN I WAS A KID my dad kept a fishing boat—an 18-footer with a cabin and a 35-horsepower "Big Twin" Evinrude—down in Florence, on the Oregon coast. We used to cross the Siuslaw River bar in that thing and troll for salmon in the open ocean. Every other trip the plugs would foul, but my father carried a spare set, and we never got stranded.

Of course back then it wouldn't really have mattered, because the Coast Guard was out there every day, along with pleasure, charter, and small commercial boats trolling for salmon; should a boat break down or the weather take a turn or the bar suddenly get dangerous, there was the Coast Guard. We never needed to be rescued, but I still remember how good it felt, knowing the Coasties were around in case we got into trouble.

Once, one of our "regulars," a charterboat operator driving a 30-foot cruiser, went out when he shouldn't have and his boat got smashed into kindling by a breaker on the bar. The Coast Guard guys took their boat right into the surf to save those people. They got to our friend first, but he waved them on to get his passengers. Unfortunately, they never found him again, but they kept on looking, driving their lifeboats through the breaking surf.

Those old Coast Guard double-ended motor lifeboats were incredible seaboats, able to take anything. A few bought at surplus were turned into pleasure cruisers and commercial salmon trollers, and I still keep half an eye out for one for sale.

Sometime in the late 1960s or early '70s, when Washington decided the Coast Guard's mission should move from maritime safety to drug interdiction, the old motor lifeboats were retired in favor of 44-foot steel boats that seem equally seaworthy, but in keeping with their new mission and its need for speed, the new boats had a broad stern, with afterbody sections flat enough to *plane*—to slide across the surface of the water instead of push through it. (If you're weak on boatspeak, see the glossary at the back of this book.) Planing takes power, but this is no problem for modern engines, which turn out far more horsepower for their weight than was thought possible back in the 1930s and '40s, when the old double-enders were in their prime.

The increased availability of harbors changed things, too. Back then, many lifeboats were launched from tracks into the surf, and they were designed to run through the surf in reverse as well as forward, and to be efficient at low speeds. And this low-speed efficiency is what makes these boats worthy of our study today. The new boats may also

■ This U.S. Coast Guard motor lifeboat is on display at the Newport, Oregon, Coast Guard base. Many of these boats have been put on shore for display, but this one is luckier than most because the local base commander made sure it was maintained. It is one of the last of its kind in good condition in Oregon.

be tremendously seaworthy, but they could never carry enough fuel to power those big engines for long-range voyaging.

For small powerboats like the Coast Guard lifeboats, unbelievable feats of seaworthiness were almost routine, and for the most part they went unpublicized. We've all read books and magazine articles detailing the grand cruises of sailors like Eric and Susan Hiscock, Lin and Larry Pardey, and Tim and Pauline Carr. But while the Hiscocks, Pardeys, Carrs, and all the others were out there sailing and writing, countless powerboats were out there, too, their owners for the most part also earning a living, but not by writing for yachting magazines.

■ A converted motor lifeboat, Coos Bay, Oregon. This craft is able and ready to voyage the world. Such converted motor lifeboats are rare and highly coveted; I know of only two north of California, although there might be a few farther south. When I asked its owner if he'd sell it, he just laughed at me.

Western America and Canada have some of the most treacherous coastline in the world, with few protected anchorages—a trip to be attempted only by seaworthy boats and mariners who are prepared. Sailing yachtsmen who negotiate this coast make a big deal of it, and rightly so. But God only knows how many 30- to 50-foot fishboats—sometimes piloted by one guy, sometimes by two, sometimes by a husband and wife, sometimes by a woman alone—have gone up and down that coast routinely. Back in the 1960s, before Government regulators killed off small family fishboats in favor of factory-owned ships, serious fishermen would start the salmon season in Monterey or maybe San Luis Obispo, and follow the fish clear up the coast into Oregon or even Washington. The wonderful old engine-powered halibut schooners ranged the entire coast. I watched one, the *Ancient Mariner,* unload a catch of squid in San Diego; three years later I saw it at the fisherman's terminal in Seattle.

At the end of one season my friends Fred and Mary cruised down into Mexico aboard their troller *Geo. Shima.* My friends Smitty and Lorraine built a 50-footer with two masts for sailing, but it also carried a 3-71 "Jimmie" diesel and 1,500 gallons of fuel. They cruised from Washington to the South Pacific and back under power, only goofing

around with sails if all the stars were in alignment.

Back in the early 1970s, my friend Jack Conway owned *Adios,* one of the most beautiful salmon trollers on the coast—and the Pacific salmon trollers were some of the most beautiful small seagoing boats ever designed. Early one spring before the season opened, Jack installed a new engine and decided to try it out, running up the coast clear to Alaska and back home to California. Now this coast is no place for small boats at that time of year. Jack said that he got into a storm, and once little *Adios* surfed a quarter mile on her side, but she got back on her feet and kept going.

I'll always admire those West Coast trollers, but it was an experience I had in Iceland a while back that really opened my eyes to the possibilities of the long-range cruising powerboat.

In 1980 I lived for three months on an island off Iceland called Vestmannaeyjar. It was spring and the sun had suddenly stopped going down, which made it really hard for me to sleep; I spent a lot of time out walking and looking around. About two or three o'clock one morning, I was down at the docks when I saw something that stopped me cold: fish being loaded from a fish plant into a little fishboat.

I have been in and around small fishboats and fishing docks a good part of my life, and I can tell you that fish are supposed to go from boats into the plant, not the other way around. So I went up to the boat—a typical Icelandic trawler: wood-built, beamy, around 40 feet, double-ended, and sexy as hell—and introduced myself to the captain.

"Sir, you seem to be loading fish. Shouldn't you be *un*loading fish?"

He explained that they were loading the fish to smuggle into England and trade for booze and electronics, both terribly expensive in Iceland. Keep in mind that this was spring in the North Atlantic, and this guy was nonchalantly going to drive his little powerboat on what the yachting magazines would call a major crossing. I later learned that little fishboats regularly chug back and forth across the North Atlantic from Iceland to England.

A few years later I made several crossings on a 45-foot Turkish motorsailer (without sails) that ferried people from Bodrum, Turkey, to the Greek island of Kos. The captain could have been Barbarossa himself. On the last trip I was the only passenger, and the Aegean was stirred up. Looking at the weather, I said What the hell; it's nice here in Turkey and we can go tomorrow. I'll never forget this man pounding his chest and saying, "I go every day!" The Turks are strong people, and this guy was indeed a manly man! Well, I figured I had the honor of America to uphold, so I went, and Barbarossa got us across just fine.

These are just a few examples of my experiences with small powerboats. And although *Cruising World* only discusses sailboats, and most people who think about "goin' cruisin'" only consider sailboats, the record is clear: Day in and day out, quietly and without attention, small seagoing powerboats prove time and again that they are proper vessels for venturing out to sea, keeping their crews safe and considerably more comfortable than they would be in a sailboat, with the crew sitting outside in the weather, trying to harness a wind that often either isn't there, or is too strong, or is blowing from the direction they want to go.

■ The fishing port of Vestmannaeyjar, on an Island off Iceland, is filled with these little wooden fishing boats, which regularly cruise across the North Atlantic to the British Isles, selling fish to the English and smuggling home electronics and booze.

Modern advertising has taken the qualities that made the small oceangoing fishboats into good seaboats and played them up as selling points for yachts. The term "trawler yacht" describes a pleasure boat, theoretically based on a fishing boat, with a deep, nonplaning hull that carries lots of fuel and has comfortable accommodations. "Trawler yacht," in modern advertising lingo, implies strength, range, comfort, and quality. Well, the virtues of displacement and solid construction, of design based on long-proven ideas of what works and is safe on open water, *are* worth bragging about. But not very many new boats touted as trawler yachts actually meet the definition. In fact, at least one is advertised as "The trawler that planes," which makes no sense to me.

At the same time, advertising for contemporary production sailboats has gone mostly in the opposite direction. The very features that make a small boat, sail *or* power, safe in open water—displacement and heavy scantlings, reliable systems, and a seakindly hull—are today considered *undesirable* in sailboats by many contemporary designers and manufacturers. Today's maritime press considers traditional safe and rugged cruising sailboat designs "second rate," yet the same concept in powerboats is written up glowingly. I've given up trying to figure it all out.

But I can answer the question posed in the title of this chapter: The long-range ocean-cruising powerboat is definitely a sensible and cost-efficient way to cross oceans, especially when compared with the typical modern production sailboat. And this isn't a new concept, but one that has stood the test of time.

A Proper
Cruising Boat

IT'S COMMON KNOWLEDGE that the proper boat for ocean cruising is a sailboat, right? Maybe. But only in very specific cases that won't appeal to most of you. There's no question that from a strictly survivalist's viewpoint, a simple, bottom-line sailboat can be cheaper, easier to maintain, and more reliable than a powerboat for long-range ocean cruising. But I'm guessing few of you would care to go that way: Although it might sound glamorous, it's neither particularly easy nor comfortable.

At this writing I'm in my late 40s, and in my life I've seen ocean cruising change from something rare and bold to something almost commonplace. Back in the 1970s, when the Hiscocks' wonderful *Voyaging Under Sail* was still the bible for ocean cruising, when the Pardeys were dreaming of cruises to come, when *Cruising World* magazine was first published, an ocean crossing in a small sailboat was sufficiently remarkable to make the local newspapers. A proper sailboat for ocean cruising in those days was moderate in beam, rig, and displacement. It was solidly built, with no elaborate and unreliable systems; sometimes it didn't even have an engine. Today this is still the safest type of sailboat—and the only type of sailboat many people can afford to own and still be able to take off cruising for a few years.

But what was sensible and mainstream just 20-something years ago isn't even talked about in today's boating press. When it was first founded, *Cruising World* magazine was so exciting: Those of us involved in the cruising life thought we had gotten a *base,* a mantra of sorts. Who would have guessed that only 20 years later it would become so establishment that it would drop its design column and write only about new production boats, which few of its early subscribers could afford and even fewer would look at twice. I don't really mean to single out *Cruising World*. The same can be said about most mainstream marine magazines.

When I was in my 20s, I went cruising in what today would be considered a "bottom-line" sailboat: simple and solid and absolutely reliable. There was no engine; if the wind didn't blow, I had a long lifeboat oar that could move it into a harbor at a half knot. At 26 feet it was a bit small, but that wasn't uncommon for a cruising boat in the '60s and '70s. It had no systems that couldn't be repaired on board, in the unlikely event they failed. It was simply and heavily built, and it was affordable. I built and paid for it while working a menial job over a two-year period, and I had the time of my life sailing it down to Mexico and across to Hawaii. Of course back then I cheerfully put up with all sorts of inconveniences and discomforts that I simply don't care to mess with these days. For instance, there was no standing headroom, no propane stove with oven. But I wouldn't trade those years for anything. When I'm 108 and drooling, it'll be to those memories that I retreat.

While there's no question that the cheapest practical approach to ocean cruising is a sailboat, it isn't the kind of sailboat you see in today's magazines, with their elaborate equipment and labor-saving devices—and price tags amounting to more than many folks will ever earn in their lives. But a simple 28- to 30-footer, with either no engine or a small one, can be solidly built of plywood or steel for less than $15,000 in 1998, and it will take you wherever you want to go in safety. And its simplicity means it will be more or less immune to the breakdowns and maintenance hassles that big-money production boats so often suffer through. It's so basic, you can fix anything that breaks yourself.

As a means of propulsion, sail is inefficient and unpredictable; you can't depend on getting where you want to go when you want to get there. But if a sailboat's engine throws a rod, eats a valve, clogs its injectors, bends a shaft, stoves up a prop, or any of the other things that are part of the powerboat owner's vocabulary, it won't stop you cold. In a powerboat, if you don't have the parts and skill to fix the problem, you're in trouble.

And powerboats will never replace the romance of ocean cruising under sail, of being completely dependent on the wind. For more than you care to learn about this, read *Voyaging Under Sail,* by Eric and Susan Hiscock. For more than you care to learn about building one, read *Buehler's Backyard Boatbuilding,* by me. I'll never knock this basic approach, because it works and it's the only way most young folks of modest means could ever go cruising. Those who do will have the time of their lives.

But us old folks won't find this approach quite as much fun. The discomforts of sitting out in a cockpit and drifting at a half knot all night in the rain didn't bother me when I was 22. But today, well, I don't want to repeat the experience. In fact, I no longer want to sit out in a cockpit at night and drive a boat at all, rain or not, even with an engine running. Today I want a cruising powerboat with a snug pilot-house and a diesel chugging along at no more than a fast idle, burning a gallon or so an hour as it pushes me along at 6 knots or better.

Cruising under power also can be pretty basic, straightforward, and trouble-free, as I hope this book will show. And luckily, just as with sailboats, the most trouble-free and reliable power cruisers are also the least expensive, which of course is why you don't see much about them in the magazines. Advertisements for cheap boats—power or sail—don't generate profits. You'll see articles about fiberglass powerboats in the 35- to 40-foot range with base prices (meaning unequipped) running past a third of a million bucks, and you'll see articles and ads for watermakers and weatherfaxes and inverters and generators and bowthrusters and all the other modern conveniences that these boats are loaded down with, but you won't see much if any design section, where new ideas are explored and the search is for a better boat, not increased profits.

But to leave off raving—and remember I'm a designer, so I take this personally—I'll finish answering the question posed at the beginning of this chapter with an unequivocal yes and no. The cheapest way to go long-range cruising is in a bottom-line, survivalist-type sailboat. But if comfort, safety, reliability, predictability, and affordability matter to you in a long-range cruiser, you're better off in a powerboat than in a typical modern sailboat. *If* it's the right kind of powerboat.

CHAPTER 3

The ~~Trawler~~
Troller Yacht

AS WE'VE SEEN, small working powerboats have for many years made ocean passages in safety and comfort. In nonworking powerboats intended for ocean cruising, the usual choice is a trawler yacht, defined as a heavily constructed, heavy-displacement hull with plenty of power, a substantial freeboard, and a high, vertical-walled deckhouse that makes it look rather shippy. But shippy-looking topsides don't necessarily mean you're looking at a real cruising boat. In 1993 I designed an aluminum 28-footer that at rest looked like a cruising tugboat, but it had a 225-horsepower outboard that pushed it close to 40 miles an hour down the Louisiana bayous, with four fat guys and one rail-thin bayou-man aboard.

There are all sorts of graphs and tables around—proportion above the waterline compared to below the waterline, horsepower to length ratios, and so on—that are supposed to explain what is and what isn't a trawler yacht. For more on this you can read Captain Robert Beebe's classic *Voyaging Under Power,* the first book ever written about long-range power cruising. In 1994 it was revised by James Leishman, and although the revision didn't hurt the basic message, I doubt Beebe would have liked its new emphasis on boats most people could never afford.

Meaning no disrespect to Captain Beebe, who practically invented long-range power cruising in the years after World War II, I'm going to ignore most tables and graphs in this book and talk mainly about concepts, some of which are quite different from those espoused by

■ Norwegian-built Romsdahl trawlers were sold in the U.S. in the 1960s and '70s. Advertised as coming over "on their own bottoms," they were made in a variety of lengths, ranging from this mid-40-footer to over 60 feet. They are beautiful, heavy-duty boats, yacht versions of typical Scandinavian fishing trawlers. This particular one, *Nor'Westing*, is based in Seattle.

Beebe and Leishman. But then the new styles of trawler yachts in the 1994 edition are quite different from Beebe's original *Passagemaker*, with its comparatively low power and low freeboard.

Speaking of low power and low freeboard, back in the 1950s there was an Aussie, one Ben Carlin, an infantryman who fought the Japanese in the South Pacific, who swore that if he lived through that insanity he'd drive a jeep on a compass course around the world. And he did, driving a war-surplus amphibious jeep powered by a four-cylinder Studebaker gas engine from New York to Alaska via the Atlantic, Europe, Asia, and the Pacific. Carlin's book, *Half-Safe*, is unfortunately out of print, but I highly recommend it if you can find a copy.

Several other people have crossed oceans in rowboats, and there was a German doctor, a survivor of Hitler's insane Russian campaign and the siege of Stalingrad, who paddled a kayak from Africa to America in the 1950s, about the same time the Aussie was out there in his jeep. I forget the title of his book, but I remember he proved that if you start drinking seawater before you become dehydrated, you won't destroy your kidneys. His biggest problem was dealing with boils on his behind from sitting in a damp kayak for weeks, but a man who had survived the Russian front didn't complain about a few boils.

Stories like these are good to read because they prove that with cruising powerboats, just as with sailboats, there are no absolutes.

You wouldn't know that to read today's boating press, for ocean cruising in a powerboat these days means ocean cruising in a trawler yacht. Some examples you might have seen are the incredible Romsdahl trawlers, made in Norway and sold in the United States in

the 1960s and '70s; and some of the Willards and the newer Nordhavens, both of which are still being built at this writing. These and other boats like them are safe, seaworthy, and solid oceangoing cruisers—no question about it.

My objection to their being held up as examples of the ideal ocean-going power cruiser is not that they aren't able, for they certainly are. But they're tanks! Their wide, deep hulls may have plenty of room, but they also need plenty of power to push them through the water. And those high, shippy-looking topsides and commodious houses have a great deal of windage.

When it comes to drag, windage is actually worse than wetted surface. A huge hull may take a while to reach hull speed if it doesn't have much power, but it will eventually get rolling along. For example, in that school that teaches tanker captains the fine points of driving a gazillion-ton ship, they use 30-foot scale models of tankers powered by 3-horsepower engines. They take a long time to get up to cruising speed (and an even longer time to stop). But they do get there. And remember: Most 30-foot pleasure boats have engines putting out closer to 300 horsepower than 3.

I learned about windage on a cross-country trip back in 1968. I was in a 1961 VW bug, with a 40-horsepower engine, a roof rack, a dog, a tomcat, a woman, and lots of stuff. At the Nebraska border we hit a head wind, and I never got that VW out of third gear until Colorado. Nebraska at 42 miles per hour—in the winter—is not

■ An unusually attractive Scottish-built fishing boat, laying at St. Katherine's Dock, London. With England's entry into the European Union, many of these boats are being chainsawed up to appease some sort of quota system imposed on the British by the EU. This seems almost a sin, as these are beautifully built heavy-duty boats.

■ The 1930s troller *Frances* has been owned for over 20 years by a husband-and-wife team. In 1996 she was one of the top salmon catchers, or "highliners" as they're called. Powered by a 3-71 GMC diesel, *Frances* ranges the West Coast from San Francisco to Seattle, going wherever the fish are, regardless of the weather. Beautifully maintained, this boat is an example of the very best in small, safe, fuel-efficient oceangoing powerboat design. A gale was forecast the day these photos were taken in Charleston, Oregon, but according to reports the salmon were thick 100 miles north off Florence, so while everybody else stayed tied to the dock, old *Frances* headed out. I asked her owner if he wasn't worried about the weather, but he said this boat easily handles it.

something I'd care to experience again.

With an ocean-cruising boat, we care less about speed than about mileage, or *range*. A trim hull with reduced windage moves easily through the water *and* the air, and so it needs less horsepower than a tank of similar size, and less horsepower means less fuel used. Good mileage!

I once had a 35-foot, 22,000-pound sailboat that I ran under power for a few months before I got around to putting up the mast.

Its little 10-horsepower diesel would push it along at 5 knots or so regardless of weather. But when I finally stepped the mast, the windage from the wires, halyards, furled sails, and spar stopped the boat cold if I tried going into the wind. The engine would chug away just fine, but the boat just kind of crawled. With the rig up and the wind blowing, that boat needed at least five times as much power to maintain the same speed.

The theoretical model for the trawler yacht is a heavy-duty commercial fishing boat, sort of a seagoing bulldozer. Its voluminous hull is beamy and high, with plenty of displacement to support the weight of the giant winches and booms that hoist the huge, fish-filled net free of the water and over the side. There's nothing subtle about the way a trawler fishes. Its mammoth engine drags a heavy net across the ocean floor, scooping up everything in its path and scraping the bottom clean. I'm surprised they haven't been outlawed.

The East Coast "draggers," as built into the early 1970s, are great examples of the type. They were built of wood, with low, seakindly hulls and small, unobtrusive houses aft. The new fiberglass and steel trawlers aren't nearly as handsome as those great New England draggers were. They aren't as seakindly either, since the designs are higher, wider, and deeper than the old-time designer/builders ever dreamed of, and their tall houses located far forward create huge amounts of windage. But then the new boats have much more horsepower than their predecessors, in part so they can tow bigger trawls to adapt to new fishing rules that open the season for only a few days, or in some cases even hours.

While the working trawler may be a rugged and seaworthy boat, it seems a poor choice as a model for a cruising boat. A trawler is designed to haul weight, to be a semistable working platform, to *fight* the sea, not flow with it. Its fat hull is designed to hold tons of fish, not the comparatively light weight of a cruising couple's worldly goods; and it needs lots of power to push it through the water. And lots of power means lots of fuel. The 1994 revision of *Voyaging Under Power* reviews a trawler yacht that burns 500 gallons a day. In the late 1990s, many folks consider environmental or cost concerns as pretty pansy stuff, but to me there's something wrong with a little 58-foot boat that sucks down that kind of fuel. Why have a cruising boat that costs that much to operate? You can travel very comfortably for $200 a day on a cruise ship, and that includes all the food and entertainment. I can't imagine, regardless of your financial situation, paying two and a half times more just for the fuel.

Earlier in this century, sailboat designers also went to commercial fishing boats for inspiration, and designers like William Atkin and L. Francis Herreshoff fine-tuned working watercraft into perfect

■ Two typical 1940s-era Oregon trollers. Note the fly bridge on *Vicki Lynn* (bottom), almost certainly added in recent years, but nicely proportioned and looking good.

examples of safe and able oceangoing yachts.

Atkin's Ingrid belongs both in the Museum of Modern Art for its beauty of line and in the Smithsonian for its brilliant statement of function. Atkin took the lines from the classic Scandinavian offshore working sailboats, famed for their symmetry and balance, and redrew them finer, more streamlined, narrower and trimmer, creating a boat just as seaworthy as the original but which moves through the water far more easily. The Ingrid is a real cruising boat, not just a rehashed commercial fishing boat. It is designed to carry a couple of people and their personal effects, not a hold full of fish and ice. Unlike most contemporary sailing designs, it has sufficient area underwater to track well and heave-to easily. It has a fully protected rudder and propeller, and a long keel that allows it to be beached or easily hauled out on small railways. Unlike some "traditional" sailboats, the Ingrid actually sails well enough on all tacks to be cruised without an engine. For the less gung-ho, 10 horsepower will get them around in calm conditions, and 30 horsepower would do in almost any situation.

That tack into sail was necessary to make a point: While the Ingrid and some other sailing yachts are highly evolved, perhaps even perfect offshore cruising boats, there are far fewer cruising powerboats with that degree of refinement. Most are pretty much just standard trawler hulls fitted out as liveaboards rather then fishboats. They're safe, roomy for their length, and have comfortable interiors. But they definitely aren't efficient long-range cruisers.

The problem, as I see it, is that powerboat designers went to the wrong fishboat for inspiration. Long-range cruisers don't need a trawler yacht; they need a *troller* yacht, a label I am pleased to say I came up with all on my own.

The West Coast salmon trollers evolved to meet criteria very similar to those of a practical long-range oceangoing powerboat. Salmon trollers don't go out like farm machinery and slowly plow the same grounds every day. They catch their fish, no surprise, by *trolling*—towing hooks and lines—and individual boats usually don't catch that many fish at a time. They don't need to. Because the fish aren't marked or torn up by nets, troll-caught salmon are the most valuable fish on the West Coast, ending up in the best restaurants and fish markets, while netted salmon end up in cans or fillets. Since they were designed to carry a small quantity of high-value salmon instead of a huge slug of low-cost fish, trollers don't need to be as fat and burdensome as trawlers. Instead, trollers are designed to move through the water easily and to cover a lot of water, while using as little fuel as possible.

Trollers frequently run for hours, sometimes even days, looking for fish. Many start the season in central California and by the end of the season range the entire coast, clear up to Oregon and Washington. And because the coast offers few harbors, they often stay out in bad weather.

In their glory days, trollers ranged in length from the low 30s, for boats that usually hung around one area, to the high 40s, for boats that wandered the coast or sometimes went way offshore looking for tuna. You hardly ever see one much over 50 feet, because they were usually operated by one person alone, or sometimes by a crew of two. Pretty much like an oceangoing cruising boat, if you think about it.

Salmon trollers hit their peak in terms of design efficiency by the 1940s. Then engine designs started changing, and power plants became available that were more powerful, lower maintenance, and most significantly lighter weight for their power output; this resulted in hull designs changing to take advantage of the new power. But at their zenith, before their fine-lined hulls began to pork-up to handle larger engines, or to be able to "cross-dress" into other fisheries besides trolling, the Pacific trollers were as close to perfection in terms of seaworthiness and efficiency under power as anything since the Eskimo kayak. Their basic concept needs very little tweaking to become the roots for a highly efficient, oceangoing power cruiser.

Think of a Troller Yacht as a Performance Cruiser, not a beast of burden like a trawler yacht. Compared with a trawler yacht, our performance cruiser is far more affordable to build, maintain, and operate; it's easily handled by a short-handed crew and perfectly comfortable for extended stays aboard. A Troller Yacht, unlike a trawler yacht, is well within the financial range of most folks with middle-class incomes.

The Affordable Cruiser

I N THE EARLY 1970S, when I was beginning my yacht design "career," I made a terrible marketing error. Not understanding why a solid and seamanlike boat had to be priced beyond the reach of working people like myself, I started designing no-nonsense ocean-cruising sailboats based, like many of the boats favored by world cruisers of the 1950s and '60s, on small seagoing commercial boats, such as the West Coast trollers and northern European fishboats. This was nothing original; plenty of designers were doing the same thing. But the times they were a changing. Small boatbuilding firms were disappearing and being replaced by production yacht manufacturers. The marine press began shifting from reader-based publishing to advertiser-based publishing. Styling trends became more important than comfort, safety, and sheer practicality. For instance, the back wall of the deckhouses on sailboats and many new powerboats began sloping forward. It may have looked racy, but it also sent rain down the companionway entrance whenever it was open, which made spending time in hot climates a real hassle. Powerboat fashion dictated a low-swept, droop-nosed profile, with no windows in the cabin. Going into one feels like you're entering a crypt.

But it was the area of materials and outfitting standards that especially concerned me. I saw friends working for years on boats, blindly following the magazines' recommendations for construction using exotic woods and all-stainless steel fittings, when I knew full well there were sound alternatives to teak and stainless that were in many cases even more durable, often just as attractive, and always far less expensive. For instance, oiled or varnished fir, oak, Philippine mahogany, cedar, pine, and many other easily found and comparatively low-cost woods make great-looking trim or interiors. Fittings fabricated from galvanized mild steel cost far less than most off-the-shelf stainless items and in many cases work better, because mild steel is less susceptible to metal fatigue. On a 40-footer, for example, a typical yacht-style stainless tube stanchion and lifeline system can cost more than $1,200, while an equally serviceable system can be made from painted galvanized pipe for several hundred. Galvanized steel exhaust parts corrode uniformly and predictably, while stainless parts look perfect one day, the next they appear pitted, and then they suddenly fail.

That stuff was just chump change, though. The big money was being thrown at mechanical and electrical systems even the U.S. Navy couldn't keep operational; there's no way a pleasure boater who isn't a mechanical and electronics genius could count on them. A friend's 38-foot motorsailer, equipped with a basic electric flushing toilet and pressure hot and cold water, rarely had both working at once. I once sailed into an isolated Mexican anchorage where a new 50-foot American yacht lay anchored. It had an elaborate sail rig, an engine room filled with battery banks, a separate generator plant, electric cooking, electric everything. It was three weeks old and dead in the water. Even its hydraulic steering system was bound up. The owners finally got a fisherman to tow them into Turtle Bay, where they waited for a factory "service rep" to fly down and fix everything. I left while they were waiting, and for all I know they're still there.

Stories like these are commonplace if you visit cruising ports, which is one reason why the best places to buy secondhand yachts are in jump-off spots like Panama, Honolulu, San Diego, Gibraltar, and the like—places where it's a long windward haul to the next civilized port with parts and mechanics.

Please don't think my emphasis on an economical approach means I'm saying settle for second best. I'm not. I have tremendous respect for the powers of Father Neptune, and I believe an ocean-cruising boat must be as reliable as possible, with systems that can be maintained and repaired by the owner any time, anywhere. But I definitely don't believe seagoing boats are the sole playthings of the wealthy. A safe, reliable, and yes, even handsome ocean-cruising boat actually costs far less than the typical tricked-out production boat. Where money needs to be spent I'll spend it. For instance, I've always bought brand-new, top-quality engines and wouldn't consider doing otherwise. The integrity of critical shipboard systems must not be compromised just to save a few bucks. But loading down a boat with the latest gadgets is neither the safest way nor even the most desirable way to go, whether you can afford them or not. I feel the "workingman's yacht" I'm talking about here is the most reliable and trouble-free kind of ocean cruiser; because of this, you'll often see boats fitting this description owned by people who can afford far more glitz but who think for themselves and intend to cruise to distant ports, where mechanics are few and far between.

Many so-called ocean-cruising boats, especially those "Gin Palaces" that never appear to leave their big-city docks—seem more like opulent motor homes than boats: machines that allow you to leave behind the comforts of home and all its conveniences without being aware that you're no longer *in* your house with all its conveniences.

When my father was in his early seventies, before he got soft and bought the pickup camper he used until his death at 86, he was camped in an Oregon state park with his little tent, his Coleman camp stove, and his cooler full of ice for his Kessler's blended whiskey. One afternoon a huge motor home maneuvered into the adjacent campsite. After it backed and filled and hydraulically leveled itself into position, my father heard the sounds of a vacuum cleaner, faintly humming over the constant growl of its electric generator. At dusk, the flickering light from a television hooked to a rooftop satellite antenna shined through its tinted windows. My father said he happened to look over and noticed two kids, faces pressed against a picture window, staring at him and his campfire. He couldn't resist; he gave them a wave, motioning them over, and the kids shot out the door and spent the evening sitting around the fire with him and talking. He always wondered if their folks ever noticed they were gone.

I don't understand why folks buy these motor homes, or their (theoretically) seagoing equivalent. A big-screen TV and a *National Geographic* nature video would serve the same purpose for a lot less money. There must be hundreds of gin palaces in Marina del Rey alone that have sat so long, their engines are seized. And I know a fine little Garden-designed sailboat that I've never seen leave its slip in Seattle's Shilshole marina in the 20 years I've been watching. Meanwhile, there's a 7-year waiting list for new slips.

COST VERSUS SIZE

ONE DETERMINING FACTOR in a boat's cost is, of course, its size. Oceans have been crossed in 6-foot sailboats, but we're talking about cruising boats here and not show-off stunts. As far as I'm concerned, if you want to be comfortable and enjoy yourself for any time beyond just weekending, a proper ocean-cruising powerboat needs a hull with enough volume to support a solid engine and enough fuel to cross an ocean. It must be shaped to move easily through the water, to be self-righting at a good angle of heel, and sound enough to take a fair amount of abuse. To me, deck space for a solid dinghy is essential, even if it's just a 7-footer. There must be enough space for a comfortable bunk, a galley with a propane stove and oven and plenty of room to cook, a place to store rain gear out of the way, and ample shelves and lockers for personal effects. But above all it must have a real wheelhouse, with a charting area, a comfortable steering station with good visibility, and maybe even a couch or an easy chair. The shortest wheelhouse that will hold all that is 6 feet, although 8 feet is better and 10 feet is ideal.

How small can you go? I could mention any size, and some guy will pop up and design something a foot shorter just to show he can. You could build a stripped-down cruiser on a 24-foot surplus lifeboat hull, but there wouldn't be much living space or a real wheelhouse. I could probably design a 30- or 32-footer that would do the job for a singlehander or a very friendly couple, but its wheelhouse would be tiny at best.

In Chapter 11 you'll find drawings of Diesel Duck 38, the smallest I think an ocean-cruising powerboat can be and still be practical and comfortable for two adults. Sure a foot or even two could be shaved off, but what's the point? As designed she's as beamy and high as I dared; were she shorter she'd need to be narrower and lower. You'd save very little in material costs, nothing in powering or outfitting costs, only 1 or 2 feet of moorage costs, and you'd loose valuable living, storage, and deck space.

How big should you go? Again, there are no hard rules to follow, except possibly financial ones. The bigger the boat, the more it costs to build, own, and maintain. Actually, 50 feet LOA seems a good upper limit, because marina fees normally take a jump at 50 feet. But if you'll be cruising much, or if you live in an area where you can simply sink a mooring for a boat, then marina fees don't figure into the equation. And if you're building the boat yourself and are on a budget, it's surprising how much big-boat gear is available surplus or second hand compared to the comparative scarcity of small-boat gear.

With the single exception of higher moorage fees, a trim, long boat is more satisfactory than a fat, short boat. Both may have the same interior volume and displacement, but the trim longer one will move through the water more easily and so will be more fuel efficient. It's likely to be a more comfortable seaboat, too. The trim, long boat's interior will be less busy than usually seen in boats its length, because a fat boat has proportionately more beam and freeboard; the lean boat's extra length allows the interior to spread out.

How big *can* you go? Who knows! When he was in his eighties, old Boyer Halverson, the Seattle tugboat legend, used to drive his 80-foot-plus powerboat around with only a 30-year-old lady cook for crew. He could turn that boat around in its own length and maneuver up to Seattle's Shilshole marina fuel dock unassisted.

Basic materials and propulsion machinery really aren't that costly. The big expense with a new boat usually comes in the outfitting. It might be fun to talk with people over long distances via a powerful shortwave radio, and with a watermaker you can take the same daily freshwater shower you enjoy at home. But neither is essential for ocean cruising, despite what the ads say.

There's also labor costs to consider. A boat that can be self-built for $40,000 can easily cost $200,000 or more if built professionally. That's not outrageous at all, but quite reasonable; and before you complain too much about the price, remember that the professional boatbuilder is a middle-class American with a right to a living wage just like you. Also keep in mind that a 25-year-old MBA is probably telling your boss right now that the firm's share prices will rise if they restructure the pension fund and downsize a few of you middle-age guys out the door. Labor is time, and time costs money.

POWER VERSUS SAIL

SPEAKING OF MONEY, the popular conception is that sailboats are more economical than powerboats. Let's look at two examples: one a 42-foot, 30,000-pounds displacement sailboat, and the other a

	SAILBOAT	POWERBOAT
Steel for hull, decks, house, tanks, and deck fittings	16,000 pounds/$4,800	20,000 pounds/$6,000
Sandblasting, insulation, paint	$1,000	$1,000
Engine and running gear	$7,000	$11,000
Mast and rigging (commercial made)	$9,000	$1,000
Running rigging, deck winches, etc.	$2,000	$500
Sails (imported; double for domestic)	$3,000	optional to $2,000
	$26,800	$21,500

42-foot, 38,000-pounds displacement powerboat. Both will be robustly built of steel; both finished to "sail/power away" status, with enough basic gear to go cruising. The powerboat has a slightly heavier displacement because, at least in smaller sizes, our performance powerboat needs to be a bit more burdensome than its sailing cousin to provide sufficient volume to carry the extra weight of fuel and larger engine. As the size increases, the displacement differential decreases, and it's actually possible for a large powerboat to be built with a lighter displacement than a similar-size sailboat. The prices listed on page 33 are 1998 retail, and they are purposely high so they'll be relevant—at least for a few years.

Most other items, such as ground tackle, emergency equipment, and the like, cost the same, whether power or sail. The powerboat will have more deck space unencumbered by booms, sails, and rigging, and so it's likely to be carrying a bigger skiff and probably a couple of bikes or even motorcycles. The house will have more glass, and if it has a two-station steering system, that will add to the cost. It will probably have a bit more room inside because of higher freeboard, and with actual cabin space (thanks to a real wheelhouse) the interior will require a little more material and time to assemble. Note that these prices include the powerboat's steadying and emergency-propulsion sail system discussed in Appendix III.

As you can see, the base materials for an ocean-cruising powerboat cost a bit less than those for an auxiliary-engined sailboat of comparable size, but on the whole, there's really not that much difference.

When we compare operational costs, however, things start to get interesting. But before we get to that, we need to talk about how people in boats smaller than cruise ships carry out an ocean passage.

If you read much about sailboats, you'll note the constant emphasis on pointing ability in advertisements, designers' commentary, and reviews. To achieve windward performance, contemporary sailing hulls are usually designed for maximum initial stability with little attention given to off-wind tracking ability or smooth roll motion. The sail plans are usually designed to drive the boat as efficiently to weather as possible, with no thought given to off-wind efficiency or short-handed handling ease.

But ocean cruising is different from afternoon daysailing or even vacation cruising. *Nobody*, except my friend Steff and a few other equally compulsive characters, sails to weather unless they simply can't avoid it. If a trip is planned against the prevailing winds, such as north from Mexico or California to Seattle, all but the most gung-ho will tack on an easy reach west toward Hawaii. When they hit the Pacific High, they'll head north and east, still on an easy reach, until they come in north of Vancouver Island or maybe even off Alaska. Then they'll head south to get to Puget Sound.

They go this far out of their way because the more direct alternative is so uncomfortable. When short-tacking, you'll cover lots of miles but not very many of them in the direction you want to go. The boat will be heeled over, which makes cooking, sleeping, and simply being aboard difficult. If there's much wind or sea, the boat will be pitching and diving, making little headway and beating up the boat and you, too.

Nobody cruises to weather who can avoid it. If there is much wind, most boats will be stopped cold by the waves. If, as is more often the case, there is very little wind, the sailboat will have to take long tacks just to keep moving at all. I've spent many 5- and 10-mile days in engineless sailboats.

I've made only two long ocean passages. One was on an engineless sailboat from Puerto Vallarta to Honolulu. The other was from Puerto Rico to Portugal on a cruise ship. Both times the ocean was more or less flat and the wind rarely over 5 miles per hour; a small powerboat could have traveled right along in a straight line, whereas a sailboat just drifted around. I have sailed off the Brazilian, American, Danish, and Turkish coasts. I've been in powerboats off the Arabian, Greek, Icelandic, English, and American coasts. I've spent lots of time around the Red and the Mediterranean Seas, the Atlantic Ocean north and south, the Pacific Ocean north and central, and various bays and gulfs scattered hither and yon. I live less than a pistol shot from Puget Sound and own a cabin on the Washington coast that sits 100 feet from the waves thrown up by winter storms. I've spent much of my life on, in, and around salt water. In my experience, the ocean is flat more often than it is rough. The problem is, of course, when it gets rough it can get *very* rough, and a boat that isn't designed and built for these occasions will eventually either kill you or at least scare you to death.

An ocean-cruising powerboat will also make its passages off the wind. Even under power, it's far too uncomfortable bucking into a sea unless you simply must. If the wind is blowing and coming from where you want to go, you likely will tack to get there. But your tacks will be closer than the sailboat's, and while you may be doing some pitching you won't be living on an angle of heel, and of course you'll be averaging a much better speed and so will reach your destination sooner. And as is so often the case, when there isn't any wind or it is very light, the powerboat will swing its nose up and head directly to where it wants to go, frequently cutting the distance traveled by a third or more.

Some intrepid folks cruise sailboats without engines, but practically all newer sailboats have fairly large engines and carry lots of fuel. A friend of mine's 55-foot ketch carries 1,500 gallons for its 3-71 GMC. Burning about 3 gallons an hour if he pushes it, his 1,500 gallons (about $1,325) will take him an easy 4,000 miles, and probably 50 percent farther if he slows down. He's powered all the way from Tahiti to Seattle, hardly using the sails, in which he probably has $20,000 invested, including the rig. That would buy 22,000 gallons of diesel at a commercial dock in the United States. The money he has tied up in his sailing rig alone would buy the fuel for more than 60,000 miles of cruising.

Sun rots sails. By the time most sailboats have cruised even half that far under sail, they're ready for a whole new suit, which for a boat his size is an easy $5,000 (imported) to $10,000 (domestic) for just the basics. If he didn't have the sailing rig with its windage, he'd probably gain at least 20 percent more mileage with the present engine, or he could use a smaller engine that would burn some 25 percent less fuel. In other words, if he had built a performance cruising powerboat, he'd be thousands of dollars ahead, and he'd have a boat that would perform better cruising the way he actually cruises.

Smitty is an old-time Northwest salmon fisherman and knows all this, which is one reason his sailboat is up for sale. Actually, he always knew that; it's just that, like so many others, he got sucked in by the boating press and built a moderate-displacement, fin-keel sailboat. It's wonderful for vacation use, but it isn't at all suited for the type of serious, long-range cruising he and Lorraine had planned.

I hope I've shown that a seamanlike voyaging powerboat really isn't any more expensive than a seamanlike voyaging sailboat, and in a long-term operational context it can actually cost less. Unless you decide your sailboat doesn't need an engine, of course. But somehow I don't think many of you would be happy with that at all.

The Case for Auxiliary Sail

THE BIGGEST FEAR folks (especially ex-sailors) have about power-boat cruising is depending completely on an engine. That's perfectly understandable. Over the years, practically everyone has had an outboard that wouldn't start and seen the occasional powerboat being towed home.

Many new boats, particularly sailboats, have engines crammed into a tiny space too cramped for easy maintenance, and their small, unprotected propellers are easily damaged by floating debris. If you've lived with that sort of nonsense, you'll be understandably cautious about putting yourself in a situation where you have to depend solely on your engine.

Back in the early 1970s, I met a guy who trolled commercially in a boat named *Raccoon*, a converted cabin cruiser completely unsuitable for open ocean work. The owner wasn't afraid of anything, though, and he took it far offshore searching for albacore and salmon. He told me a story I'll never forget.

He was several hundred miles off Los Angeles when his engine died. Ships and even other fishing boats were in the vicinity, so he wasn't worried. He got out his flare gun (back then many small boats didn't carry radios), and whenever he saw a boat he shot off a flare. Either nobody saw him, or nobody was willing to help him.

Several days went by, and he finally realized he was on his own. From the low mast that supported the trolling poles, he hung a makeshift sail made from bedsheets, towels, and whatever else he

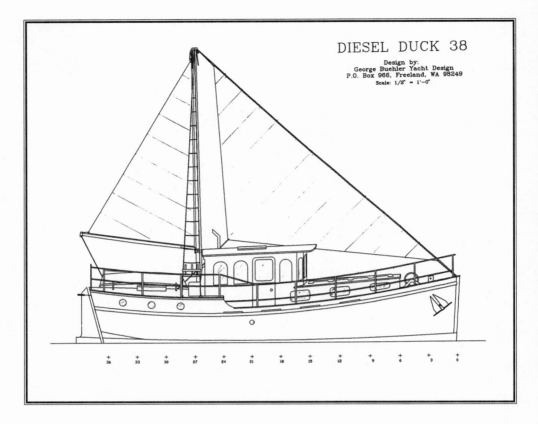

DIESEL DUCK 38

Design by:
George Buehler Yacht Design
P.O. Box 966, Freeland, WA 98249
Scale: 1/2" = 1'-0"

36 33 30 27 24 21 18 15 12 9 6 3 0

■ This sail plan won't win you any races, but it will absolutely guarantee that you won't be left drifting helpless like a jellyfish should your engine quit. It also dampens roll, increases range, and can serve as a cargo-loading system.

could find, but because his boat had absolutely nothing in common with a sailing hull and had just a typical powerboat's little spade rudder, which works only when the prop is pushing water past it, he had absolutely no control and ended up going backward at about a knot toward the middle of Baja California. After several days of this, a friend of his came by and stopped to offer a tow. The guy said he was so pissed off about his situation and the previous lack of assistance that when he saw his friend's boat coming, he went into the cabin and didn't want to come out. He had resolved to crash onto a beach in Baja then *walk* back to California. In the end, of course, he accepted the tow back to San Pedro.

Stories like these remind us that big problems can happen, but they can happen whether your boat is sail-dependent or power-dependent. Sailboats can be dismasted; even the popular unstayed sailing rigs have been dismasted, despite the hype you read in the ads. A powerboat completely dependent on its engine can stop cold. A backup engine can be put out of commission by a tankload of bad fuel—which is far too easy to encounter in far-distant ports. Sure there are chemicals that keep fuel from going bad, but they don't convert bad fuel into good fuel. Sure you'll be carrying extra filters and will have a fuel system designed so that you can clean it, but what do you do when the problem rears its head far from port and a source of new, clean fuel, and you're drifting helpless?

Given clean fuel, a modern marine diesel is almost completely dependable. If you pay attention to maintenance and religiously monitor the gauges, those engines will run forever, with no problems you can't easily fix shipboard. But if you stop and think about all the things that must happen to make that engine run—all the parts in there going up and down and round and round, squirting fuel and lube oil and circulating water and releasing gas and turning a shaft and prop that might at any second hit a log or wrap around some loose driftnet and bring everything to a stop—you'll just shake your head and wonder why in the world you ever thought of going to sea.

Stupid stuff can happen! Once I was driving across Wyoming in a snowstorm at 20 below, when a rock bounced up and hit my radiator. The little four-banger Mercedes diesel overheated and stopped me cold. Luckily another car came by before I froze to death, but I never forgot that. Who would guess you could overheat an engine at 20 below zero?

To my mind it just makes no sense to rely completely on engine power, which is why I won't go into any detail about pony engines or chain drives off the genset and so on; if you want to read about that stuff, there's plenty of other sources.

When I go to sea, I want a top-quality marine diesel engine, fully accessible in a real engine room, with a religiously observed maintenance schedule, the best filters, a complete set of spares for the impellers, fuel lines, filters, belts, hoses, and whatever else I can fix without a machine shop, and a complete set of spares for the spares. But I've still got to have one last backup that will never fail: *sails*.

You can hang a sail on anything, but as my Baja-bound friend found out, that doesn't mean it will sail. Most powerboats—especially trawler yachts—are so high, wide, and burdensome that their superstructure alone has more square footage than any auxiliary sail rig you could carry; sailing in any direction other than directly downwind would be impossible. But our Troller Yacht is different: Even though it isn't really designed for sailing, its hull form isn't that far away from a heavy-duty working sailboat. With a small auxiliary sail rig, a Troller Yacht could sail as high as 90 degrees into the wind. So what if you can't short-tack up a channel; at least you'll never be reduced to drifting backward toward a beach 300 miles away. You'll have enough control, thanks to the big rudder and sail plan designed with off-wind propulsion in mind, to set a course and actually get where you want to go. And in port, you can use the boom to hoist aboard your skiff or motorcycle.

If you remember my earlier tirade on the perils of wind resistance, you may be thinking that the spar and boom and rigging for even a low sail plan creates an awful lot of windage. It does create some, but its benefits more than compensate. The mast and rigging's windage and weight aloft actually slow the boat's roll. At anchor, the spar itself will dampen the motion; at sea, a boat with a steadying sail set will roll far less than the same boat without one.

The original Diesel Duck had a mast and steadying sail smaller than the one shown on page 38 (it wasn't rigged for sail assist or back-up), yet even that was enough to make the boat "comfortable" on a trip down the California coast with 11-foot seas. It was also enough to serve as a riding sail and would hold the boat's nose toward the wind when anchored or if the owners wanted to heave-to and fish. A lot of the lobstermen in Maine do this, setting riding sails off the stern of their 30- to 40-foot boats so the bow stays into the wind while they haul back lobster traps. You'd think the small West Coast crabber or shrimp-pot fishermen would rig this way, but maybe they don't have the comparatively recent tradition of working sail that the Maine guys do. Although you'd think they'd have thought of it by now.

Some of the West Coast old-timers still rig steadying sails on their deep-water fishboats. Once in a while you'll see one on a troller, and the big halibut schooners that every spring leave Seattle for the Bering Sea still carry two masts, both able to hoist a low sail.

The old-time rigs stand out against the big modern boats rigged with "flopper-stoppers." These are paravanes that dangle from port and starboard booms when the boat is at rest or underway; they do reduce rolling, but at the cost of a great deal of windage (and expense) from the complicated rigging and about a 10 percent reduction in range, from the drag of the vanes being towed through the water.

Flopper-stoppers do dampen roll better than a sail if you're in a heavy swell with no wind. There's a partial solution if you're anchored: Tie a big weighted canvas bag, with a spacer to hold it open, to a 15-foot rope; attach that to the end of the boom, then swing the boom 90 degrees off the side of the boat. If you're underway, however, there isn't much you can do.

But then, of course, a flopper-stopper won't get you home under sail if your engine conks out, and in most cases steadying sails not only dampen roll but also help propel the boat, saving fuel and greatly increasing range.

Some boats, especially those with deep, round, roly-poly hulls, such as the Romsdahl trawlers, reduce rolling with permanent fins, similar to sailboat bilge keels. Some new trawler yachts even have hydraulic stabilizers, similar to those seen on cruise ships. A hired captain I know told me he won't take the 72-foot yacht he runs offshore without the stabilizers, because the boat is so top-heavy he's afraid of it.

Bilge keels might not be a bad idea, especially on steel boats, but to me, hydraulic stabilizers are just one more complicated and expensive system to buy and maintain and have break down at the wrong time. And like flopper-stoppers—and unlike a simple steadying sail—they're no help at all if you want to heave to and ride out a storm, or simply drift and fish, or, of course, get back to shore if the engine dies.

The Engine

THERE'S AN OLD SAYING that goes something like, "For want of a nail a shoe was lost, for want of a shoe a horse was lost, for want of a horse a kingdom was lost...." The point this sort of illustrates is that, while we might think the most important part of our ship is the engine, it really depends on the circumstances. If the engine fails, the backup sails are the most important. If the weather gets rough and you find yourself cowering on the wheelhouse floor, the hull is the most important. If the engine quits and you take a 360, and the mast goes and you're drifting helpless like a jellyfish, then the water tanks are the most important. An ocean-cruising powerboat is a combination of important systems, and equal thought, care, and planning must be given *all* of them.

By the way, *don't* call an engine a motor. A motor is powered by electricity, springs, or hydraulic fluid. An engine converts combustion energy into mechanical force or motion. Calling an engine a motor is like calling frames ribs. It's lubberly!

Incredible engines are available these days. At this writing I'm working on the design of a 45-foot Florida day boat powered by a turbo-charged and intercooled 300-horsepower diesel. It's an engineering marvel—compact, lightweight, high output, and no bigger than the 350 Chevy V-8 in my car. And a perfect example of what you don't want in an ocean-cruising powerboat. The problem is, it's designed to run at high speed; it doesn't even begin to run efficiently until it's putting out around 100 horsepower. This is fine for a planing hull or a light semiplaning hull, but a displacement hull can't use all that power. In normal running, our 40- to 50-foot ocean-cruising powerboat rarely uses more than 30 horsepower and frequently less. Bucking into heavy weather demands more power, but since this is almost as uncomfortable in a powerboat as it is in a sailboat, it's something we normally avoid.

A high-speed engine in a displacement hull can't run fast enough to operate efficiently. Compared with a heavy-duty, slower-turning industrial engine, the high-speed engine will cost more, use more fuel, will have a shorter life, and demand more maintenance.

And don't even think about a gasoline engine. There are some good ones available, but gasoline has several disadvantages for a seagoing boat. Compared with diesel, gasoline is an inefficient fuel. A gallon of gas produces about 10 horsepower for one hour; a gallon of diesel produces about 20 horsepower for one hour, meaning a diesel gives you twice the range per horsepower. Diesel fuel is also cheaper than gasoline most places in the world; it's far more available in out-of-the-way ports, and is far less explosive than gas. But the most important problem with gas engines is their electrical ignition system. Electrical stuff doesn't like salt air; if moisture gets into the ignition system, if the battery dies, a spark plug fouls, or a lead gets shorted by dampness or vibration, the engine stops running. Diesel engines are far more reliable. Since diesel fuel ignites by compression, not by an electric spark, diesel engines need electricity only to run the starter.

Some diesels don't even need electricity for that. Compressed-air starters aren't uncommon, and some old European fishboats use a system where you heat the cylinder head good and hot with a blowtorch, stick a 5-foot pry bar into the flywheel, give it a push, and the engine starts. This is really neat to watch! Other engines of older design, like the Norwegian Sabb, start with a hand crank, and in cold weather you add a special starting "cigarette." Light one, stick it in a hole in the cylinder head, and after it's warm you can easily start the engine with the hand crank. In the case of a Sabb at least, it has to be damned cold before you even need to bother with the cigarettes. I had a Sabb in a sailboat and could easily hand-start it even in freezing weather.

It's easy to poke fun at these old-time systems, but you know, they work, and they're so simple they're foolproof—far more so than modern engines. To start in cold weather, the five-cylinder diesel in my old Mercedes, like most modern diesel engines, must heat its cylinder head with electric glow plugs. This is reliable, but it isn't foolproof; a lot can go wrong with a battery, glow plugs, and the circuitry that activates them. Once, I couldn't start the car until I figured out that while the fuse in the system was good, the contact points the fuse rested against were corroded.

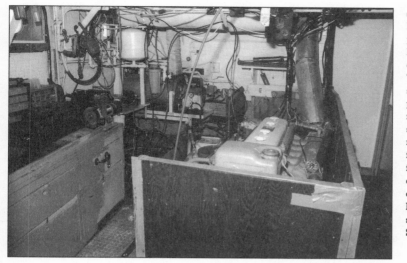

■ The Detroit Diesel 71 series is perhaps the biggest selling diesel ever made. They are inexpensive, easy to get parts for, and very reliable. Note the spacious engine room, which is 10 feet long by the full 12-foot width of the boat. There are shelves and benches on all sides. Photos by Stacia Greene.

Sabb has a clever advertising slogan that goes something like, "Norwegian nostalgia is a developing country's progress." A long-range cruiser has a lot in common with a developing country. There is just no way an engine can be too simple to operate or maintain; the simpler the systems are, the more reliable they are—and the more likely you'll be able to fix something if it fails.

Today, few engines are designed specifically for marine use. Most are industrial models, originally used in tractors or trucks but "marinized," either by the factory or by an after-market dealer. "Marinizing" means adding a water-cooled exhaust manifold, and perhaps altering the tuning, injectors, and cam to make the engine more efficient at the long periods of constant engine speed characteristic of a boat. This places much different loads on an engine than does a tractor or a truck,

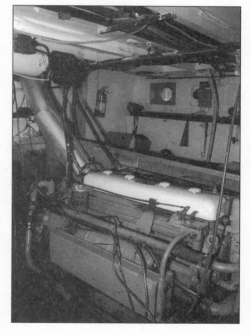

but most industrial-type diesels can handle this fine. A good first step in investigating an engine's suitability for marine use is to see if the same engine is offered as a stationary generator plant. If it has the guts for this, it has the guts to drive a boat.

The big-name American engine makers—Cummins, Detroit Diesel (GMC), Caterpillar, Ford, John Deere—all make wonderful engines, well proven by countless hours of use in commercial boats, long-haul trucks, and industrial generating plants. These companies make full lines of diesels, but we're only interested in their smaller, naturally aspirated models, meaning not turbocharged. A *turbo* is an air compressor driven by exhaust gases that crams in combustion air and produces far more power per cubic inch of engine displacement than a naturally aspirated engine. Turbos even reduce fuel consumption, but I still wouldn't want one on a long-range cruising boat. Turbos are pretty reliable, but they are still the one engine component most likely to fail, and repair parts can be hard to find, especially in the kinds of places most of us want to cruise to.

It's hard to pick one brand name over another; all have wonderful reputations and loyal followers. Where I live, some folks like Ford pickups but most prefer Chevys. Nobody likes Dodges, but that's all I'd ever own in a pickup. For all this brand loyalty, they all seem to work about the same (except I think my Dodge works a little harder).

The original 38-foot Diesel Duck (see page 145) used an 80-horsepower Cummins; it was far more power than the boat needed, but it never missed a beat. Cummins is an old-time company—a big name in boat engines and a huge name in truck engines. Two friends replaced the 6-71 Detroits in their dump trucks with six-cylinder Cummins and they love 'em, claiming more power and lower fuel bills.

John Deere engines are really coming on strong in the marine market. A Seattle company started marinizing them years ago, selling them under the name Lugger. Around 1990 the Deere company, seeing the wonderful reputation Lugger had created for them, began selling their own marinized version for a bit less money. The Lugger people believe their marinizing package is better, but both share the same Deere engine. Deere is known for its low fuel consumption, reliability, and longevity. A few years ago, John Deere ran a clever advertising campaign featuring a couple of old codgers sitting on a porch speculating about "just how long does a John Deere run?" My father loved that commercial. It reminded him about when he was a kid, growing up on the family farm. They used to rig a battery light on their John Deere, with its big steel wheels, and work shifts plowing 24 hours a day; that tractor was never shut off in planting season. After 15 or 20 years his father—suffering from farmer's disease, which requires new machinery to medicate—sold the old Deere to a son-in-law and it ran for years and years. My father said *nobody* knows how long a John Deere will run! I know of a 1930s-era Deere that was dredged out of the Columbia River and resurrected.

Robert Beebe used a Ford in his famous *Passagemaker* and never said anything bad about it. Ford diesels are popular fishboat engines, both in Maine and in the Canadian maritimes, running year-round in mostly lousy weather. The original Alcina 48 (see Appendix I) uses a six-banger Ford.

The Detroit Diesel (formerly General Motors) 71 series is perhaps the biggest selling diesel ever made. In use since 1938 (with more than 300,000,000 documented running hours by 1980), these engines are certainly well proven. The "71" means each cylinder has 71 cubic inches (there are also 53, 92, and 149 series); in "6-71," the "6" means six cylinders. The 71 series used to be made as small as a 1-71 and as big as a 16V-71, which has two banks of eight cylinders. The V-16 in my friend's Alaskan crab boat runs almost continuously for two years at a pop, then is shut down and given a thorough looking over during a summer refit. In 1996, the Seattle Detroit Diesel dealer told me the company had dropped the one- and two-cylinder models and is offering only the three-cylinder model for generator plants. The 6-71 is a bit large for most of us, but the two smaller models are just about right. Countless 35- to 50-foot fishing boats use the 3-71, and countless 40- to 60-footers use the 4-71. Tens of thousands of these engines were built over the years, and you can buy a rebuilt 3-71 or 4-71 for around $4,000.

Jimmy Diesels, as they are affectionately known (or "Screaming Jimmies," as they are less affectionately known), are two-cycle engines; most other engines are of four-stroke design. Two-strokes have fewer engine parts, and each piston downstroke produces power; with a four-stroke, every other downstroke produces power. This is why serious dirt bike racers like two-strokes: instant response. Two-stroke diesels burn slightly more fuel than four-cycle engines, but because these things have been made so long and are so widespread, you can find parts practically everywhere in the world, and most guys with the nerve to say they are diesel mechanics have experience working on them.

Along with the 53 series (53 cubic inches per cylinder, 73 to 173 horsepower), GM has a series of lighter engines—the Bedford diesels, made by GM England—that run from 49 to 109 horsepower. Unlike other GM diesels, the Bedford is a compact, fairly light four-stroke, and it's less expensive than other engines in the line. I recently talked with a guy who has a six-cylinder Bedford in his 45-footer and loves it. I was struck by how pleasant its exhaust sounded—an odd observation I know, but an important one if you're going to be living with the noise for days at a time.

Many lesser-known companies also make good engines. The German Deutz, available in both water-cooled and air-cooled models, is a wonderful engine, as is the British Gardner. Deutz, being German, has a pretty good international dealer network. Gardner is considered one of the best engines ever built, but since it's British you have to search for one. British business practices are far too subtle for me to understand; there's no dealer network, for one example, and they downplay their products, for another example. A client of mine recently called Gardner to ask which model they'd recommend for a Diesel Duck. The factory said they don't recommend any of their engines for ocean cruising, and what's more they think ocean cruising in a powerboat is a dumb idea. I like British people fine and own a number of British products, but I'll never understand how they stay in business.

Hundesteds, from Denmark, are also great engines. Each is made to order, is frighteningly expensive, and will last you the rest of your life. Hundesteds are a real old-time design: a single cylinder, huge flywheel, very low RPM.

One of my favorite production engines is the Norwegian Sabb. The 30-horsepower model is a two-cylinder workhorse—114.7 cubic inches, 1,900 RPM, 836 pounds, with compression releases and a big heavy flywheel so you can hand-start it. The factory recommends this engine for pleasure boats that make between 6 and 9 knots, as an auxiliary in sailboats to 55 feet, and for workboats to 35 feet. An average 35-foot Norwegian workboat is a heavy-duty trawler tub, which indicates that this engine is satisfactory for Troller Yacht–type boats up to the mid-40-foot range. Several people are building Diesel Ducks at this writing and using the 30-horsepower Sabb.

I enthusiastically recommend these engines. Although Sabb has no dealer network, you can call the factory in Bergen, Norway (53-34-35-10), give them a credit card number, and in a month or two the engine will arrive at your door; they arrange everything, even customs.

Other good engines are around, and just because I didn't mention one you like, don't let that stop you from buying it. Parts availability is a major consideration, but international telephone calls, credit cards, and worldwide express shipping mean that even a small company with no international dealers can service you quickly anywhere in the world. It might be hard to find a mechanic familiar with more obscure engines, and you might have to wait a little longer for parts, but that wouldn't stop me from buying what I like. For instance, a few years ago I bought a 32-horsepower three-cylinder Lister. Parts have to be shipped from the factory in England, but it's a wonderful engine and I like it. Besides, with good maintenance, it's highly unlikely that a heavy-duty engine like this will ever need parts until it has accumulated thousands of hours. Even then, if you plan a major overhaul *before* the engine actually dies, it's a simple matter to order the parts, go wherever you need to find qualified help, and plan the rebuild for a time you want to do it.

It's easy to decide when an engine needs a rebuild, or for that matter to accurately estimate a secondhand engine's condition. Most major cities have testing labs (look in the Yellow Pages) that can analyze engine oil for trace metals. This costs less than $20, and the printout will tell you exactly how much of what internal part is worn. When X percent of Y shows up, it means the bearings are bad or the cylinder walls are wearing or whatever.

Oil analysis makes buying a used engine less risky, but if I were spending the money to build a new boat, I would think twice about installing a secondhand engine. Even if the basic engine is perfect, there are many incidental parts that will stop you dead if they fail. One is the injection pump; you want one that is new or at least rebuilt. Same with the starter, especially if you can't crank-start the engine.

Trust me on this: Saving a few hundred bucks on an engine will likely come back to bite you in the tail. Your long-range powerboat is essentially useless without a completely reliable power plant, so don't stint. Buy either a new engine or one completely rebuilt by a very reputable shop, with a real business address and a track record. I had one engine rebuilt by a very good backyard mechanic. He did a few things wrong, didn't stand behind his work, and I had absolutely no recourse other than shooting him, which had repercussions that weren't worth it. That engine ended up costing me more than if I had gone out and simply bought one from a dealer, and the one from the dealer would have worked perfectly; if it hadn't, it would have had a guarantee I could depend on.

How Much Power?

YOU KNOW YOU NEED AN ENGINE, but how much engine? Not an easy question; there are just so many variables in how engine output is listed. First, the advertised horsepower is rarely the real horsepower but instead a measure of the maximum power the engine can develop. And if you run it at that power for more than an hour, you'll likely blow it up. Actual usable output is called *continuous-duty horsepower*, typically 20 percent less than the advertised horsepower. For instance, the Detroit 3-71 is rated at 113 horsepower but 82 *continuous* horsepower.

The dictionary defines a *horsepower* as "a unit for measuring engines, where 1 horsepower equals 746 watts or 33,000 foot-pounds per minute." A *watt*, named after James Watt, the inventor of the steam engine, is defined as "a unit of work done at the rate of 1 joule per second." A *joule* is defined as a unit of "energy equal to the work done when a force of 1 newton acts through a distance of 1 meter." A *newton* is "the unit of force required to accelerate a mass of 1 kilogram 1 meter per second per second." A foot-pound is "the work done to a force equal to 1 pound when it acts through a distance of 1 foot in the direction of the force."

■ A four-cylinder Cummins fits nicely in the 6-foot by hull-width engine room in the Diesel Duck 38. Note the dry stack, well insulated with a fabric heat shield, and the sound-deadening material on the overhead and forward bulkhead. Photo by Patricia Blackshaw.

All these definitions seem to indicate that a horsepower is a horsepower, but when you compare engines of similar horsepower ratings but of dissimilar sizes, the measurement no longer make sense. For example, a Yanmar 1GM10 is rated at 9.1 horsepower at 3,600 RPM, measures 19.41-cubic-inch displacement, and weighs just 167 pounds. The same-size Sabb produces its 10 horsepower at 1,800 RPM, measures 46.3-cubic-inch displacement, and weighs 441 pounds. The Yanmar is a fine and popular auxiliary engine for small, light sailboats. Sabb recommends their 10-horse for use in displacement powerboats to 25 feet and as an auxiliary in sailboats to 37 feet. I've seen it used as an auxiliary in a 20-ton, 43-foot sailboat. One of the first transatlantic powerboat crossings was in the 1930s by a Swede in a 32-footer powered by a 10-horse engine, certainly a Sabb or something very similar. I've used the 10-horse Sabb in a 22,000-pound 36-foot sailboat and found it had plenty of power to push me at near hull speed into anything, until I put up the mast and it came up against all that windage.

To further confuse matters, industrial and marine engines are rated both in horsepower and in *kilowatts* (equal to 1,000 watts); this is the preferred rating method in Europe and Asia. If all this is even more confusing, at least kilowatt ratings provide a nonsubjective measure of power. My Mister Coffee is rated at 1.25 kilowatts no matter how much it weighs. The 9.1-horsepower Yanmar is rated at 6.7 kW, and the 10-horsepower Sabb is rated at 7.3 kW.

Horsepower can be developed either by a little engine spinning fast or by a large slow-turning engine with the mass to develop *torque*, which is defined as "a force that creates a wrenching or twisting effect." A slow-turning, high-torque engine, with its big, heavy flywheel, powers a long-range cruising boat more efficiently than does a high-speed engine of the same horsepower because it can twist a bigger propeller.

A propeller screws its way through the water the same as a wood screw goes into wood. All things being equal, a big propeller turning one revolution will push a displacement-hull boat farther through the water than will a small prop turning one revolution.

Propellers for planing hulls have a different set of realities. A planing hull is shaped to skip across the top of the water and needs a small prop turning really fast to get it up on plane. If the hull won't plane, the prop will just *cavitate* (the prop loses its bite on the water by turning faster than it can push water past) at higher RPM. Hang a new 10-horse outboard on a 20-foot work barge, open it up, and its little two-blade prop spins and spins while the hull slowly accelerates to hull speed. Hang on a 4-horsepower Seagull, with its big, slow-turning five-blade prop, and the barge will quickly accelerate to hull speed because the prop is turning slow enough to bite into the water, and the prop is big enough to push a lot of water.

Displacement boats almost always use a reduction gear to reduce the speed at which the propeller turns; this allows the engine to operate at its most efficient speed while turning a larger prop with more twist to the blades (*pitch*) than it could if it turned the prop at the same speed as the engine, or 1:1 (say *one to one*). The slower the prop turns, the more pitch there can be to the blade; and the more pitch (the wider the threads of the screw, so to speak), the more water it pulls through it each time it rotates. The most common reduction ratio is 2:1 (two revolutions of the engine to one revolution of the prop shaft, or screw). The smaller the engine, the bigger the reduction gear needed in a heavy boat. I have a 3:1 gear on my 32-horsepower Lister, and I've seen a 4:1 gear on a six-cylinder Chrysler car engine mounted in a 45-foot workboat.

The Norwegian Sabb has an interesting system. The engine comes with a built-in 2:1 reduction coupled to a variable-pitch prop. This is a little more fragile than a normal fixed blade, but you gain added control over your power. You can give it full pitch and cut back the RPMs in calm conditions, or cut back on the pitch and rev up the engine when you're bucking wind and wave, similar to downshifting a car to run up a hill. And when you twist the blades backward for reverse, you get a hell of a lot more power than you do with a normal fixed-blade prop running backward. That Sabb 30-horsepower diesel and prop system is really something. Don't get me wrong; I love my Lister. But if I hadn't been offered a half-price deal on it, I'd own the Sabb.

So how big of an engine do you need? Well, there really are no hard-and-fast rules, but there are some things to base your guesstimates on. First, we need to determine where and how we'll use the boat the *majority* of the time. Since the subject of this book is long-range cruising, let's start there.

You'd plan a cruise in a small powerboat along the same lines as you'd plan a cruise in a sailboat. No one will want to spend much time going against the weather because it's simply too uncomfortable—the sailboat will be on its ear and the powerboat will be bashing into it. Therefore you'd choose your courses so that the prevailing winds put you on a comfortable reach.

With sailboats, this means that a really good cruising rig is designed less for pointing efficiency than for off-wind performance, although you'd never know this reading the boating press, which emphasizes pointing ability above all.

The Troller Yacht faces exactly the same realities. No matter how much power you pour into a displacement hull like this, it will never go more than a few knots faster than its hull speed. We know that it takes only minimal power to move a boat like this in calm and off-wind conditions, and since this describes the majority of our travel, we'll rarely need much more than minimal power. Of course a Troller Yacht is quite different from an actual working troller. Look at the photographs of *Frances* on page 24. She's heading out of harbor *into a full gale* because the owner heard the salmon were biting 100 miles up the coast. If you plan to earn a living trolling, you go where the fish are, regardless. But you and I just aren't going to do that. We might be heading up the coast and run into a full gale, but we'll be happy to slow down and take things as smoothly as we can. The owner of *Frances* can't be so casual, yet even this serious, all-weather, 42-foot, 45,000-pound-displacement workboat has only a 3-71 Detroit rated at 82 continuous horsepower, and the owner told me this engine is more than satisfactory.

It's far better to have a smaller engine running at an efficient speed than a big engine throttled back to just above idle. A 30-horsepower engine that usually runs at 15 to 20 horsepower will be happy; it has a bit of a load on it, it's running warm; oil and fuel are flowing through it at a nice rate, keeping everything lubricated. A 100-horsepower engine running a long time at 15 to 20 horsepower won't like it, because none of the things that make the little engine happy are happening. You'll need to run the larger engine fast enough to keep it happy, which means you'll usually be developing more horsepower than the hull actually needs to move, which means you'll be burning more fuel than you'd need to burn.

Of course sometimes it's good to have raw power. If you're primarily cruising areas with strong tides or if you're specifically planning a route that runs into the teeth of the normal weather, then you'll want an engine with the reserve power to stand up to things. But most of us aren't planning those kind of uses; we'll be cruising off-wind in calm weather, for the ocean is calm more often than it is stormy. We don't need much power.

The table above shows theoretical power requirements in calm

33-FOOT WL, 28,000-POUND DISPLACEMENT, D/L = 347

V/L	SPEED (KNOTS)	HORSEPOWER
1	5.74	4.3
1.1	6.03	5.6
1.2	6.89	10.5
1.3	7.45	19
1.35	7.76	25.9

40-FOOT WL, 35,000-POUND DISPLACEMENT, D/L = 244

V/L	SPEED (KNOTS)	HORSEPOWER
1	6.32	5.9
1.1	6.96	9.1
1.2	7.59	14.4
1.3	8.22	26.2
1.35	8.54	35.6

48-FOOT WL, 58,000-POUND DISPLACEMENT, D/L = 234

V/L	SPEED (KNOTS)	HORSEPOWER
1	6.93	10.7
1.1	7.62	16.4
1.2	8.31	26.1
1.3	9.01	47.5
1.35	9.35	64.6

conditions for three different hulls. Notice how little power is actually needed to move them at hull speed (1.34 V/L). Since we'll normally be cruising at 1.1 or 1.2 V/L (speed-to-length ratio), enough power to hit 1.34 should be plenty, even though it may not be enough to buck into a full gale.

TWIN ENGINES?

ONE ENGINE OR TWO? The advantages of a twin-engine cruiser are well known: You get the safety of a backup power plant; you have a built-in parts storage house, because you can cannibalize one engine to keep the other running should they both quit; and you get tremendous close-quarter maneuverability. But the disadvantages far outweigh the advantages. For starters, your expenses double. Aside from buying two engines, you'll also need two rudders, two shafts, two props. Since neither the shafts nor rudders are on the centerline, they'll be exposed to hitting things unless protected by skegs, which adds to the construction costs. If you don't have skegs and you hit something like the trees that float around Puget Sound, you'll certainly lose at least one shaft, prop, and rudder, and probably all three. If you're really unlucky you'll sink when the rudder breaks off the hull.

Fuel consumption will certainly be higher with two engines. You may be running both engines at a lower RPM than you would one, but you're still running two engines. If you try to run on just one, the drag from the stationary prop will make you run the one engine harder than if you just had one engine. Maintenance doubles, too. Two cooling and exhaust systems, double sets of filters, and on and on. No way!

If you're worried about close-quarter maneuverability with a single-screw installation, just go down to a busy fishboat harbor and watch those guys sling their boats around effortlessly. That's because they know how! The big props grab the water; the big rudders steer when the boat coasts in neutral; the hulls have enough underwater area so they aren't blown sideways. With practice you can do it, too. But if you're really worried about close-quarters maneuverability, install a bowthruster. Maneuverability is even better than with a twin-engine rig, and a bowthruster is considerably less expensive than a second engine.

And if you're worried about relying on only one engine, remember that sail is a reliable, never-fail backup system. If you're on a tight budget, sails and a bowthruster together still cost half or less the cost of a second engine. And if you're especially paranoid or really hate sails, then there's no reason not to install an air-cooled Lister or Deutz somewhere near the shaft, rigged up with a chain sprocket. This will get you home if the main engine dies. But there's absolutely no reason to install any other kind of twin-engine installation in a Troller Yacht. And that's all I'm going to say about it.

Design
Considerations

THE LONGER THE BOAT, the lighter its displacement can be in proportion. Thus, designing a Troller Yacht with sufficient volume to carry a livable interior and enough fuel to go places is a challenge in shorter lengths. The 38-foot Diesel Duck is a good example of how compromises are made to create a smaller design that is still relatively trim. With a D/L of 313 she's a hefty little ship, although still far less bulky than the average trawler yacht her length, the D/L of which ranges up to around 500. She has sufficient volume for a comfortable two-person interior, a real engine room, lots of fuel, and scantlings heavy enough to hit things and live to tell about it, all in a short overall length. The hull may be a bit stocky, but at least it doesn't look like something from a bubblegum machine. While pushing the boundaries, she's still fairly trim.

THE HULL

THERE ARE NO HARD-AND-FAST RULES about boat design, which is more art than science and more compromise than either. Still, a number of generalities have over time proven to be good ideas for all offshore displacement boats; following them will ensure your Troller Yacht does the job you want done.

Foremost is *seaworthiness*. A boat that can't be trusted in bad weather is just no good. Never mind about the engine and the interior

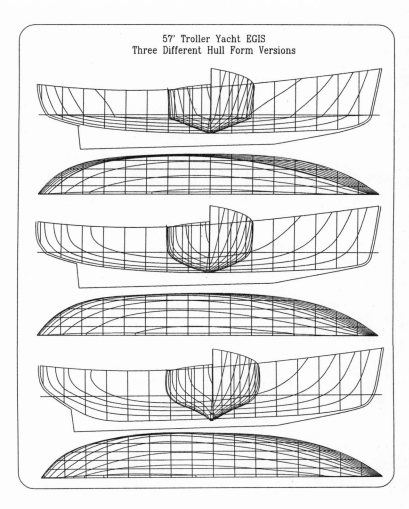

57' Troller Yacht EGIS
Three Different Hull Form Versions

layout. The hull itself must be able to deal with the ocean in all its vio-
lence. If you're ever so unlucky as to blunder into a Godawful tropical
hurricane, you want to feel there's at least a chance of staying afloat.
Modern sailboat design has gotten so far away from this basic tenet
that a book was written about it. C. A. Marchaj's *Seaworthiness: The
Forgotten Factor* was a big seller and widely discussed in the sailing
press. Yet the quest for speed under sail still leads manufacturers to
make their boats ever lighter. And people buy them.

Seaworthiness centers around structural integrity. Fuel efficiency,
speed, and cost all pale compared with the basic design requirement
that a boat not break up at sea. Although we want to keep down hull
volume in an efficient cruising boat, it still has to be heavy enough to
support the weight of a serious construction plan. A cruising boat
must be built *stout*. Forget the theoretical strengths of the materials;
pay no attention to calculated stresses. A cruising boat must be built

57' EGIS HYDROSTATIC CALCULATIONS FOR THREE DIFFERENT HULL FORMS

	HARD CHINE	ROUND BILGE	ROUND BILGE, HOLLOW GARBOARDS
MAIN DIMENSIONS			
LOA	56.45'	56.45'	56.45'
LWL	53.18'	53.43'	52.37'
Beam	14.36'	14.35'	15.59'
WL Beam	13.72'	13.63'	14.57'
Hull Depth Less Keel	3.31'	3.37'	4.24'
Volume	877.27' 3"	956.79' 3"	1,058.16' 3"
Displacement	57,145 lbs	62,234 lbs	68,720 lbs
COEFFICIENTS			
Prismatic	.614	.596	.605
Block	.374	.389	.327
Midships	.609	.654	.541
Waterplane	.708	.694	.672
RATIOS			
L/B	3.88	3.92	3.59
D/L	167	179	211
Lbs./Inch	2,754	2,697	2,730
CENTROIDS			
LCB	52.2% aft	52.6% aft	54.4% aft
LCF	54.3% aft	54.0% aft	54.5% aft
VCB	−1.05'	−1.16'	−1.33'
MOMENTS			
Trim 1 inch	7,725.8	7,362.5	7,171.3
Trim 1 degree	86,376.8	82,706.9	78,876.0
Heel 1 inch	1,912.2	1,750.6	1,756.4
Heel 1 degree	5,514.2	5,016.3	5,378.9
AREAS			
Waterplane	516.35' 2"	505.65' 2"	511.84' 2"
Wetted Surface	610.56	601.37	637.77' 2"
Total Hull Surface Area	1,249.52' 2"	1,253.37' 2"	1,294.34' 2"
STABILITY			
GM trans	5.63'	4.69'	4.55'
GM long	88.15'	77.39'	66.73'

stout, which I define as a boat with enough big pieces so that you look at its construction plan and say, "Damn, this boat is built *stout!*" I realize how unscientific this sounds, but there's no other way to put it. This is important! If you look at the construction specifications of a modern steel or aluminum design, you'll usually see the work of a calculating engineer and not that of a complete coward who has spent time at sea. You'll see steel yachts as long as 60 feet designed with a 1/8-inch plate hull. Sure, a 1/8-inch-thick hull backed up with longitudinals will keep out of the water, but if you come down on a rock or hit a log, you've probably lost the boat. You don't want your hull strong enough. You want it *strong*!

A good hull must be inherently *stable*; it must want to float rightside up. Robert Beebe made up something he called the Above/Below Ratio to quantify the proportion of hull above water to that below water. The idea is, you want enough hull below water to keep the part above water, *above* the water. Again, there are no actual rules other than observation. The hull needs to be deep enough so you can look at the drawings and get the feeling that she is *in* the water, not sitting on top like a leaf. Of course there are exceptions.

A Saint Pierre Dory is very seaworthy, at least when handled by a helmsman who knows what he's doing; they were fished commercially year-round from the Saint Pierre and Miquelon Islands, off the southern tip of Newfoundland—not exactly a millpond. These boats have a flat bottom and a very shallow draft (they were hauled ashore through the surf after fishing); they also have very low freeboard and are quite narrow along the bottom, with extreme flare to the sides and a high bow and stern to lend great reserve buoyancy. Because of this configuration there's no room inside, and they make poor cruising boats unless you really stretch them out. This can be interesting, though. I've been sketching out some ideas along this line and have come up with Pilgrim, the 44-foot cruising dory shown in Appendix I. She looks able enough, although in bad weather you won't feel as secure as you would in a conventional Troller Yacht. Still, one of these Dory Yachts would be extremely fuel efficient and very simple, inexpensive, and quick to build.

A cruising hull needs to be *seakindly*. That's another vague term, but it means a boat is happy in the water. A good hull looks like it's riding in the water, not bobbing around on top. A seakindly boat has "easy" sections, which give it a smooth rolling motion rather than making it jerk back and forth, which is what happens with a hull with a really "firm" midsection shape.

The sectional shape needs to have some vee, or *deadrise,* as it's called; and to retain our "easy" hull form, the degree of deadrise remains similar as length increases. Deadrise also adds to the displacement, since the more hull (volume) below water, the more the hull needs to weigh to support that submerged volume. Longer boats need less displacement to support the hull's scantlings and provide a comfortable interior and can thus become narrower and shallower in proportion to length. This is where the difference between a fuel-efficient Troller Yacht and a conventional trawler yacht becomes obvious; the longer the hull and the finer its lines, the easier it slides through the water.

There are two distinct hull types: the common, traditional round bottom and the less common but just as traditional *chine,* or V-bottom. While chine hulls aren't seen often with sailboats—although the earliest chine hulls I know of were Viking ships built before A.D. 1000—they are very common in powerboats. Along the Chesapeake Bay, folks claim single-chine hulls date back to Indian times, and today their traditional workboats still feature single chines. Throughout the Gulf of Mexico, single-chine hulls have long trawled for shrimp in all kinds of weather.

A single-chine hull and a round-bottom hull with similar, fairly deep deadrise perform very much the same. The big difference is in construction costs. A single-chine hull can be built in roughly half the time as a round hull, especially in metal or plywood. With one-off fiberglass or ferrocement construction it makes little difference, except that, because of the nature of the material, single-chine fiberglass has a built-in weak spot at the chine corner. That's easy enough to solve, of course: Just build up the corner.

Lacking a reverse curve aft, a single-chine hull does have less room in the after part of the bilge, but the cost advantages of the single-chine hull are so great that if you need room in the aft bilge, you'll be money ahead stretching the boat 10 feet longer. The payoff for the extra length will be better performance and more room for about the same money. I like single-chine hulls and believe they are every bit as good as a round-bilge hull. My only criticism is cosmetic: Single-chine hulls don't have the flowing good looks of a round-bilge boat, especially if they have a transom stern. Keeping the freeboard moderate helps avoid any awkwardness in the chine hull's appearance, however, and with a double-ended hull, both types look almost the same. Don't dismiss chine hulls, especially if construction cost is an issue. There are many highly successful single-chine boats out cruising today. Power *and* sail.

Bulbous bows are a common affliction on new production boats, especially Trawler Yachts. Bulbous bows were developed for oil tankers to help control pitching and to increase hull speed with a fully loaded ship (they detract from performance when the tanker runs light). So while tank testing might show that a bulb protruding from the bow below the waterline has some effect in some circumstances, those same tests show that the bulb detracts from performance at speeds other than the one for which the bulb was designed. Even if you think you'll be running the boat at that speed 95 percent of the time, its effect is too minor on boats smaller than a full-size cargo ship to justify the extra cost of building the bulb. One very experienced boatshop owner told me that the bulbous bow on the steel 60-footer his shop was building added three weeks to the construction. The owner could have added 8 feet or more to the hull for less money, and this would have had an easily measurable and dramatic effect on performance, not to mention living space.

Every designer has a different opinion on this subject, so here's mine: Bulbous bows have a positive effect with ship-size hulls that always run at a certain loading and speed. For cruising-boat-size hulls, however, which run at many different speeds and degrees of loading, I think they're nothing but marketing hype. If bulbous bows do such great things for displacement-speed hulls, as some boat factories claim theirs do, wouldn't we see them on racing sailboats? I think a bulbous underwater protrusion on the bow of a small boat is ridiculous.

Hull *symmetry* is important. A good seaboat hull has similar areas forward and aft of the midsection, both below and above the waterline. Visualize a beer bottle rolling on the floor. It's symmetrical and so rolls in a straight line. Visualize a light bulb rolling on the floor. It pivots on its fat butt and swings its nose around in a circle. This symmetry of ends is far more important with a cruising sailboat, because when heeled, an asymmetrical boat doesn't want to steer a straight course. A powerboat doesn't heel like a sailboat, but it does roll back and forth with normal swells; a symmetrical hull rolls smoothly and won't try to change course as it rolls, making it easier to steer. This is particularly important in such common cruising conditions as running downwind in the trades. With the continuous 20-knot trade winds, the ocean will be lumpy, and even with our steadying sails doing their job, a hull that can't roll in a line parallel to its keel will give you an uncomfortable corkscrewing motion.

Hull symmetry can save your life when running in breaking waves; a narrower, symmetrical-ended boat is much harder to broach than a wide boat with an unbalanced hull. Cruisers hope to avoid this situation, of course, but sometimes you can't. For instance, crossing a river bar can get hairy fast; not infrequently, boats broach and are driven right up onto the rocks. Actually, one of the safest boats for crossing a breaking bar is a fast planing hull—as long as the engine doesn't quit. I've crossed a breaking Oregon bar in a planing hull, riding the back of a breaker with another breaker hanging almost over the stern. We were perfectly safe as long as we had the speed to keep up with the waves, but if that V-8 Ford had missed a beat, that would have been that.

Symmetry shows in two places. The *center of buoyancy* (CB) is a calculation that tells us how the underwater area is distributed. For a cruising boat, the CB should be close to the hull's midsection. The farther toward one end it is (usually the stern), the less symmetrical the underwater area is.

This calculation doesn't say a thing about the topside areas, however, so here you have to use your eyes. If the deck view is fairly similar front and back, then the volumes of the topside area are similar. Double-enders are the easiest to check out, but a transom hull with a full bow and a high transom can be very close to double-ended at the waterline. An extreme example of hull symmetry is a gravel barge. Another is Joshua Slocum's old *Spray*, with its huge transom and bluff bow.

Asymmetry is designed into powerboats to get a broad stern area that will support the hull in a plane or semiplane. Asymmetry is designed into displacement hulls to gain extra room for the interior or to come closer to a semiplane, allowing the boat to exceed hull speed if you've got enough power on board (and don't mind spending a lot of money on fuel for a modest increase in speed). Our efficient Troller Yacht can't begin to semiplane, so there's no reason to choose an unbalanced hull other than to gain the interior room a wide stern provides. But it's foolish to compromise the seaworthiness of a symmetrical hull to gain interior accommodations; if you feel you need more room aft, build a longer hull.

This basic rule of symmetry is important for all offshore displacement boats. Many new trawler yachts (and new fishing trawlers, for that matter) have abandoned symmetry to gain interior space, but if you study old-time hard-core working trawlers like the great New England draggers or their European cousins, you'll see that while they're all burdensome and heavy, they're also all symmetrically

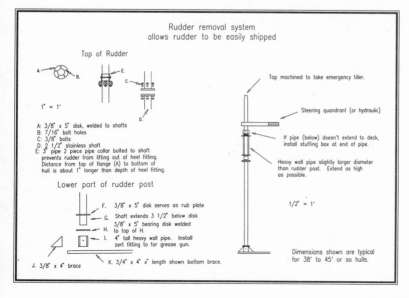

■ **Rudder removal system.**

ended. And finer seaboats have never been built.

Finally, a good cruising hull must be designed to meet basic cruising requirements. It must be able to run aground or be careened on its side for painting or maintenance without being damaged. Hitting a coral reef in heavy surf will raise hell with the best of boats, but hitting a sandbar or even coral in calm conditions shouldn't be a big deal. This requires a long, solid keel. If the hull is fiberglass or wood, the keel and bow must be faced with a heavy steel shoe.

The rudder and shaft must be protected. A safe seaboat shouldn't have a strut and exposed shaft and rudder, so if you're planning to ignore my advice and install twin engines, you'll want two deep skegs to protect all that exposed stuff.

And any serious cruising boat needs a rudder that can be easily removed. This isn't commonly seen in yachts, probably because most production builders, looking to cut costs, don't bother installing the flanges required to make shipping an inboard rudder an easy job. But if you have rudder problems in a remote location with no marine railway to haul your boat, you'll be glad you have an easily removable rudder.

DECKS AND DECK STRUCTURES

THE MOST SEAWORTHY BOAT ever built is a submarine. Equally safe above the water or below, long and narrow, with no deck structures or windows to break, a submarine can deal with anything. A sub can be blown up or wrecked, but no sub since the first wooden tub powered by a hand-cranked screw has been overcome by the ocean itself. Maybe the distant future will bring us cruising submarines, but today our Troller Yacht is the next best thing—about as safe as a small boat can be.

With all boats, the primary areas of weakness are the deck and its structures. Windows and cabins simply aren't as solid as a smooth hull. Most of the time this isn't a problem, but those of us who worry about everything that can happen are the ones who are prepared *if* it happens, so we give lots of thought to the deck structures.

Ideally, we want a low profile to minimize windage; we want minimal large, flat surfaces that can be knocked off the hull; and we want no large windows in a position to be broken by heavy seas. All-steel or aluminum construction minimizes the risk of losing a deckhouse, but windage is still an issue, as is losing windows.

As always, how the boat will be cruised must be considered in the design phase. A boat based mainly in placid climates won't need the same attention given to cabin and window area as one headed for the

■ Forward of the Diesel Duck pilothouse looking back (top), and inside the Diesel Duck pilothouse looking out (bottom). Photos by Pat Blackshaw.

high latitudes. Still, a boat planned to be reasonably suitable for high latitudes will provide an extra measure of safety anywhere.

There aren't any rules for deckhouse design, other than basic and obvious proportional considerations. For instance, a 40-foot hull with three deck levels will be top-heavy, and that huge deckhouse will be fragile. I'll assume that anybody reading this has some

idea of the proper proportions for cruising boats. If you don't, look at some older commercial boats designed to work offshore.

Our Troller Yacht must be sufficiently comfortable to live aboard for extended periods, but not at the risk of compromising its safety on open water. It isn't a motor home or a houseboat, and it doesn't have the volume of a trawler. It's a trim, *traveling* seaboat, and its deck structures will be smaller than those on many modern yachts.

■ The 72-foot *Aquavit* pilothouse has a generous 12-foot-long floor and is 8 feet wide. This large pilothouse allows plenty of room for lounging. The dinette table drops down to make a guest double bed. Looking forward (top) and looking aft (bottom). Photos by Stacia Green.

The strongest possible way to build a deckhouse is not to build one at all but to build a *raised-sheer* or *flush-deck* design. The hull sides are built a little higher and windows are let into the hull sides, with additional light and ventilation provided by deck hatches. Flush-deck design provides the most interior volume because there are no house walls or deck carlins. It's also the simplest to build.

A flush-deck boat also provides the maximum deck space, although a low deckhouse with a handrail and wide side decks can ease getting around in bad weather. Of course that's more of a sail-boater's concern; in bad weather us powerboaters are in the pilot-house. A low deckhouse allows you to install more windows without weakening the structure than you could in the hull sides of a flush-deck boat; you can also achieve a lower apparent profile, and the house floor can be a little higher above the bilge, giving more space for storage and tanks.

Like everything else in yacht design, this is all a trade-off. The compromise I like best is a flush-deck, raised-sheer design from the stern up to the pilothouse, with a low deckhouse forward of the pilothouse. I frequently use this deck design even in large boats because it's very practical and I like the look.

Dinghy storage is a consideration. A flush deck aft provides a good, safe place to lash down a decent-size skiff without it's being in the way or interfering with visibility. And you want a decent-size skiff. Years ago I carried a 5-foot 8-inch pram—all that would fit on my small cruising sailboat's deck—and I've had it with small dinghies. Today I like a skiff I can step into without tipping the damned thing over, and that means at least a beamy 10-footer; 12 or even 14 feet is better.

The *pilothouse* needs a lot of thought. It must be high enough to see what's in front of you but low enough to minimize windage. And a cruising boat's pilothouse should *be* a pilothouse. Make it big enough to serve as a substitute lounge, and it adds too much windage and has so much surface area that it could be damaged or even busted off in heavy seas. Also, if you're running at night and have any interior lighting turned on, you can't see out the windows; using the pilothouse as a galley or main lounge would be very difficult other than at anchor, since you'd have a choice between seeing where you're going or seeing what you're cooking. The galley and lounge area should be completely separated from the steering area.

The space below the pilothouse is the obvious spot for the engine room in most boats. Six feet seems to be about the minimum length for an engine room where everything is easily accessible, and a 6-foot floor in a pilothouse can be quite spacious. An 8-foot floor is luxurious, and makes for a commodious engine room below. The shortest floor I've seen was 3 feet, but even that worked pretty well because there was a built-in couch behind the steering station to provide more room. Regardless of the floor length, the forward wall of the pilot-house will extend onto the forward deckhouse roof 2 feet or more beyond the floor, and the back wall can also extend over the deck or sternhouse top. This provides both added shelf space and easier access to the forward and aft cabins.

INTERIOR

YOU CAN DO ANYTHING YOU PLEASE with your interior. This freedom is one of the best reasons to build a custom boat. As with everything else about a boat, you need to consider how you'll be using the boat most often, then design an interior tailored for that use.

Easy access to the *engine room* seems an obvious requirement but it's rarely seen. I want a real door to my engine room, maybe even a small window so I can glance in occasionally. I don't care for engine-room access through lift hatches in the floor, except to provide full access for major maintenance or engine removal. If a lift hatch is the sole access, however, getting to the engine is just too inconvenient to glance in casually whenever you feel like it. I was recently aboard a new $360,000, 42-foot production boat that had the silliest engine access I can imagine. You lifted a hatch in the cockpit (advertised as the lazarette), pushed aside all the stuff that normally fills a *real* lazarette, then dropped down and crawled along 15 feet forward, almost on your belly, to get to the 450-horsepower turbocharged Cummins. I asked the broker if he really thought the Retired Republicans this boat was marketed to would put up with, or even be able to make use of, that kind of access. He didn't say anything.

A cruising boat needs full, convenient, safe, and *immediate* access to all parts of the engine—none of this leaning over the top to reach things. The engine needs to sit up proud and happy, with at least 18 inches between it and anything else; 2 feet or more is much better. You need enough headroom to move around easily; you don't need full standing headroom, but slithering around on your belly in an engine room is ridiculous. You need shelves and racks to conveniently store tools and parts and whatnot. It's good to have space for a small workbench with a vise and a hand-operated grinding wheel. This isn't a sailboat, with its infrequently used engine tucked away out of sight. Our entire boat is based around the engine, and the engine room must be well thought out and big enough to work in.

Guest accommodations are, to me, one of the most common mistakes in long-range cruising-boat design. Far too many boats pack in bunks for the occasional guest while robbing the owners—typically a couple—of valuable living space all those times when they don't have company.

Our Troller Yacht is meant for ocean voyaging, but even the most ardent voyager will likely be in port a majority of the time, so unless you plan to stay ashore whenever you're in port, you should plan the interior around your concept of comfortable living. My particular personal life demands a double bed, preferably queen-size. Five by 7 feet is luxurious, especially in a boat; 4 feet is the minimum for a double, and 4½ feet is a good compromise. I also want a desk or a table for writing or crafts, and a comfortable seat.

I like this "bedroom" in the stern, because this is one of the most comfortable areas in the boat (other than the middle; but for mechanical, access, and weight-distribution reasons, the engine gets that), and because this moves my bedroom as far from the engine and other living areas as possible. This makes the bedroom quieter, and more important, it makes it a completely separate part of the boat, a place where someone can go and be alone. This is important on a long-range cruising boat; you'll start hating even your dear old mother if she's always in sight.

Sometimes you'll see this "owner's cabin" tucked up into the bow, usually because there isn't much space there for anything else. The disadvantages of this location are a lack of floor space due to the narrowness of the hull there, meaning you can't walk beside the bed (how soon we become spoiled), and the extreme motion of the bow area when underway or at rough anchorages. Usually I put the head forward, since the head area is used less often than any other part of the interior. In larger boats the bow makes the best place for guest bunks. Even then, I suggest using folding bunks so that when you don't have company, you can use the cabin for something useful, like an office or a shop.

You want a real *kitchen* (I'm avoiding the nautical word *galley,* which to me means a cramped cooking space tucked into a corner) with a big counter, a propane stove and oven, and a big sink. I used to like double sinks, but I'm beginning to suspect that a really big single sink is more convenient. Because a Troller Yacht spends a lot less time on its ear than a sailboat, a normal house-type sink should work fine; I don't see the need for a deep (expensive) sailboat-style sink, although they are a good place to tuck the stewpot should the weather turn nasty.

It's good to have a large table with comfortable seating, ideally with outside visibility. This table can convert to a double bed, solving the guest accommodations problem. Comfortable seating in the main living area is great, but in smaller boats the table area will probably be the only place with the room for this. The pilothouse itself can have a built-in couch or an easy chair so that it doubles as a lounge, as long as you remember that this is first and foremost a steering station.

For some reason, most new boats seem to have *multiple bathrooms.* We all have our phobias, and while I am compulsive about many things, I don't feel anxious whenever I'm farther than 20 feet from a toilet. Most of these bathrooms that look so good on the yacht salesman's accommodation plans are miniheads, so cramped you can barely turn around. Instead of a separate shower room, they provide a curtain that supposedly blocks the spray; this rarely works, with the result that the toilet paper and towels and everything else in the bathroom gets damp whenever you take a shower. And these curtained-off shower areas are rarely bigger than 2 by 2 feet, so the shower curtain ends up sticking to you.

I can't live that way. A liveaboard interior should provide at least the same comfort level as we'd demand in a studio apartment. To me, a large, convenient bathroom is essential. I like it to be 4 feet wide or better yet 5 feet, and at least 4 feet deep, with a real counter and shelves. The shower should have its own room and be at least 32 by 32 inches; 3 by 3 feet is much better. On larger boats I even like to see a small bathtub! A decent, convenient bathroom makes long-term living aboard actually comfortable rather than just something to put up with.

Finally, give some attention to *handholds*. The boat is frequently moving—rolling, diving, pitching—and negotiating a huge open floor area can be treacherous because there's nothing to lean against. A narrow floor makes things safer inside because you can't fall very far, but where a narrow floor doesn't fit into the design, be sure you have a convenient handrail or a post to grab on to.

This interior I've described sounds pretty Spartan when compared to many new boats. If you look at advertising brochures you'll see all sorts of really clever uses of space, with stuff built in all over. But in real life a lot of this just doesn't work because nothing is really big enough: the bunks aren't quite long enough or wide enough for comfortable sleeping; the galley counter doesn't have enough room for a real cook to work; you bang your elbows in the toilet room; you have to crawl into the engine room; and on and on.

No thanks. If you plan to spend much time aboard a boat, the interior has to be laid out to meet your living needs, as comfortably and conveniently as possible.

Construction Materials

FOR A VARIETY OF REASONS, one of the variations of steel or wood construction will be the most practical choice for building a one-off boat—bearing in mind, of course, that even as you read this sentence someone is probably building or cruising in a boat made from something else entirely. Before deciding on a building method, add into the equation a material's availability, familiarity, and your own prejudices, because in boatbuilding as in so much else, few things are carved in stone. While there are certain design and structural considerations you should not treat cavalierly, a custom boat can be whatever you want it to be, no matter what you build it from.

That being said, I should mention that I am an unashamed, unrepentant, and *proud* Wood Boat Man. I've been one since I was a little kid, and my stubborn German blood keeps me one today. Wood just makes a "nice" boat. It's an insulator, so wood boats are quiet and dry inside. And I love looking at a wood boat's structure. The deck beams, the knees, the bolts—all combine to form an internal ambiance unmatched by any other form of construction.

WOOD

WOOD IS A GOOD CHOICE if you're building a boat yourself. Although looking at a finished boat may make you think building one is an overwhelming chore, a wood boat goes together one

■ First-time boatbuilder Fred Hammond erecting frames on his wood-hull 48-foot Alcina. Photo by Fred Hammond.

piece at a time, and if you ruin one piece of wood you can saw out another. Wood isn't the most practical choice for hiring the boat built, because it's labor intensive and demands skilled (read expensive) labor. But wood is a great choice for a home builder because each piece is light and easily handled, wood is easy to shape and fasten together, it's very clean and relaxing to work with, and if you have the skills and tools for basic home maintenance or building a doghouse, you have the skills to build all but the most complicated hull. No matter what kind of hull you're planning, you'll almost certainly build the interior from wood, and building a simple wood or plywood hull actually requires less skill than building a wood interior.

Wood is a living thing and to me boats are living things, and I believe that a Living Boat should be assembled from a Living Material, piece by piece, even though I know how obsolete and impractical that sentiment is today.

I was lucky enough to be born while wood boats were still the norm, and I was especially fortunate to have spent several years in Maine in the late 1960s working as a floor sweeper and general wood butcher for several top wood yacht-building firms, working on such grand projects as a replica of the schooner *America* (105 feet long, double-planked fir hull, sawn oak frames, teak deck, Everdure and bronze fastened) and a Herreshoff-designed Ticonderoga. Large-scale wood yacht-building ended just a few years later. Goudy & Stevens, the wonderful old-time yard that built the *America* and many other fine yachts, went under in the early 1990s. The other yard I worked at, Paul Luke, saw the way the world was going, switched to aluminum construction, and is still going strong.

But wood itself isn't what it used to be. These days it's hard to imagine a tree so fat it takes a whole Peterbilt to haul just one small section, but when I grew up in western Oregon, a log truck loaded down with just one log was a common sight. I remember that, and I remember the wood from those grand old trees—boards that were clear and tight-grained and strong. People built their houses using only clear, vertical-grain wood, and the boats? Well, the boats were built from the very best wood of all. The finest trollers and schooners were planked with wood cut high up in the mountains, where the cold weather slowed tree growth; the slower the growth, the tighter and stronger the wood. The finest sailboats had spars cut from Washington's San Juan Islands, where the winter winds blow so strong only the hardiest trees survive.

Even though I saw it happen, I still find it inconceivable that in the span of 30 years all this disappeared: the huge 1,000-year-old trees, the rivers clogged with log booms, the uncountable little sawmills and wood boatyards and the lifestyles they supported. It's hard to imagine now that boat-grade Douglas fir boards have become so rare that they cost $4 a board-foot (1 × 12 × 12 inches), and at that price rarely of top quality.

Even in the 1960s, foresters were saying that West Coast timber was being cut faster than it could replenish itself, but few people believed this and even fewer cared. The timber companies had a simple philosophy: Get the timber and damn anything else. Forests were leveled by the square mile, with only a thin buffer of trees left along the highways to shield the clear-cuts from view. I first saw a clear-cut—I mean really saw it—in the summer of 1981. I drove around a corner in the Olympic National Forest and there was what looked like a World War I battlefield—not a tree for miles, the earth torn up as though by an artillery barrage, broken stumps and limbs and small trees tossed every which way. It was the most devastating and ugly thing I've ever seen. If you care to see just what has happened and continues to happen to our forests, take a commuter flight from Seattle to Portland, or from Portland to Grants Pass.

■ Building outdoors in Ontario, Canada, Fred Hammond finished the composite wood hull, deck, pilothouse, and many of the mechanical installations for his Alcina in two years. Photo by Fred Hammond.

In 1980, when Ronald Reagan became president and James Watt (who said publicly that he was expecting the Second Coming any time now and knew Jesus would want to see that we had used the earth's resources) became secretary of the interior, the deterioration accelerated. With the reduced regulations, combined with a tax code and emerging corporate ethos focused only on quick profits, timber companies began exporting raw logs. Trucks drove right past American mills closed for lack of timber, right through neighborhoods filled with American citizens who once worked at those mills, hauling our timber to be loaded into ships and carried to Asia. In 1990, a Columbia River bar pilot told me that at least three ships loaded with timber crossed the Columbia bar alone every *day,* and this was common in ports up

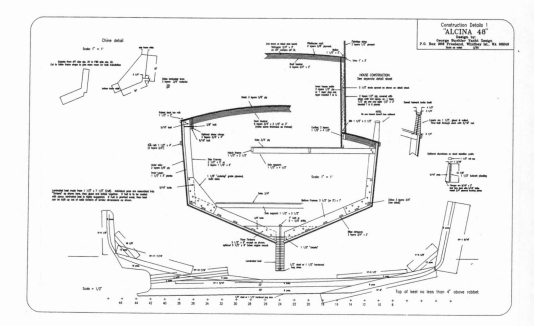

Construction Details 1
"ALCINA 48"
Design by:
George Buehler Yacht Design
P.O. Box 966 Freeland, Whidbey Isl., WA 98249

■ **Wood construction Alcina 48, cross-section view.**

and down the West Coast. In the mid-1980s, there might be more log ships on any given day in little Everett, Washington, than there were merchant ships in Seattle.

This mass rape is still going on but not nearly as extensively. Despite the best efforts of the 1994 Congress to turn back the clock, the laws are finally tightening up, and of course the forests we once had just aren't there anymore. State and federal timber may no longer be exported, but private companies still do it. Last week I was down at Hoquiam on the Washington coast and saw the old Mayr Bros. mill shut down and an auction notice nailed on the fence. Meanwhile, the harbor is stacked high with timber from private land, all waiting to be loaded onto ships bound for Asia. I don't know how those longshoremen and truckers and local shipping people have the nerve to walk the streets of their community.

Of course transferring blame is always easier than admitting responsibility, and around these parts the politicians and private timber companies like to blame the Endangered Species Act in general and the spotted owl in particular. You see a lot of hand-painted signs in timber communities saying "This business (or family) is supported by timber dollars." I keep meaning to nail up some signs along clearcuts that say, "Look! Another place the spotted owl stole my job!" And while many timber-dependent people are blind enough to believe their problems are all caused by tree-huggers and a bird, I know a lot of former loggers and millworkers and fishermen and boatbuilders who understand that politicians and rabid talk-radio hosts have used

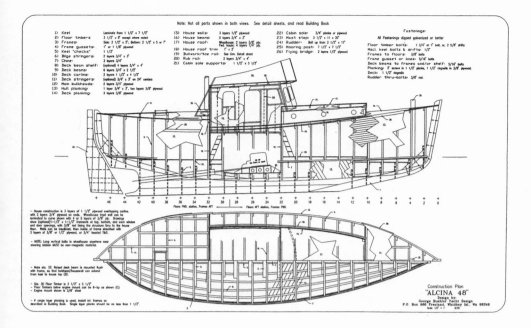

■ Wood construction Alcina 48, full construction plan.

the owl as a convenient shield for their own irresponsible management and greed.

It's not that those of us whose lives are associated in some fashion with healthy forests care about the owl in particular; I understand owl tastes like chicken. But there's a point that should be obvious to anyone: If there ain't enough forest for an owl to live in, there sure ain't enough forest to saw down and ship to Asia.

This socioeconomic commentary was a necessary preface to discussing wood as a hull material, because since the 1970s, the nature of wood boatbuilding has changed considerably.

With the demise of the great forests, the easily obtainable and affordable first-quality wood also disappeared, with the result that today's wood boats are often built of materials our forefathers would have hesitated to use in a good house. Of course some traditional plank-on-frame hulls are still being built, and I hope they always will be. But since the 1980s, new glues, epoxy coatings, and preservatives have revolutionized wood boatbuilding, and with the use of plywood, laminated timbers, epoxy saturation, and other composite construction techniques, modern wood boats live long lives and require less maintenance compared with those built with traditional wood construction methods; in fact, the new techniques actually produce a boat with lower maintenance costs than metal and far more pleasant maintenance than fiberglass.

Setting aside the sappy emotional stuff, modern wood construction has many advantages. Wood is easy to maintain. I find annual sanding and painting far more pleasant than the annual buffing and waxing required to keep a plastic boat looking good. You can repair a damaged wood hull anywhere, and unless you've gotten smashed on a reef and suffered a major structural collapse, you can patch even a large hole, in the water, with materials easily stashed below a bunk. Wood has greater abrasion resistance than fiberglass. Wood is the only construction material that doesn't fail after prolonged flexing. Wood isn't bothered by temperature extremes as fiberglass is. Ever see a Corvette that got hit by a rock in very cold weather? The body shatters! And wood is stronger than steel for its weight, although of course as steel gets thicker it rapidly becomes stronger, and 1/4-inch steel will deflect light-caliber gunfire.

Wood does deteriorate over time, and the stuff available today won't—without some attention—have the lasting qualities of wood from the old days. But wood rot doesn't just suddenly appear and destroy everything in its path. In fact, if you pay attention to proper ventilation and use preservatives, it's unlikely to get started in your lifetime. Salt water itself is a preservative, and a plywood deck coated with one of today's miracle materials, and that has good scuppers that don't trap rainwater, will keep the inside dry and free of fresh water, which is what causes rot.

If you poke around the corners and hidden spaces once a year or so, you'll spot any potential trouble areas well before they become a problem, and can easily fix them. If you do find some rot, you can either cut it out or, believe it or not, saturate it with common automotive antifreeze, which displaces the moisture in rotted or waterlogged wood but never evaporates. Marine archeologists use antifreeze to preserve shipwrecks hundreds of years old that, if allowed to dry out, would turn to powder. That's a good tip for home repair, too, by the way.

Finally, wood boats are fun to own because of all the wood boat stuff you can participate in. There's wood boat festivals all over the place, and although the wood boat crowd is often a touch holier-than-thou and maybe just a bit snooty toward powerboats, they are on the whole good people and their festivals are always fun. A new wood boat makes you feel part of a select few, although frankly *any* custom boat gives that feel. But the wood boat scene encourages that stuff and what the hell, it's harmless and kind of fun.

Unfortunately, while there's always a small market for wood yachts, their resale value in general is low, they can be harder to sell than anything else this side of cement, and some insurance companies won't touch them.

STEEL

STEEL CONSTRUCTION MAKES a lot of sense. It's certainly the strongest way to build. A heavy steel hull will take just about any abuse. If it bangs into rocks or washes up on a beach, it might get dented but it probably won't break up. A steel deckhouse welded to a steel deck is permanent. A capsize or rogue wave might take out all the glass, but it won't dislodge the house itself.

Steel yacht-building has been common in Europe since the earliest part of the 20th century. In the States, commercial boats have been built of steel for years, but steel yachts are a recent addition.

In Europe, many steel hulls are assembled very much like wood hulls, with closely spaced transverse frames to which plating is welded. European builders tend to use designs identical to those used for traditional wood boats—even round-bottom hulls with reverse curve to the garboard area. This is an extremely difficult way to build in steel; the hull plating is normally quite thin, and it's hard to weld the thin plate to the frames without getting that "starved horse" look, where the frames show clearly from outside the hull.

We Americans (and I believe it was West Coast Americans) developed another method. The frames support longitudinals and can be spaced anywhere you want; normally I specify them spaced at 3 feet 6 inches, just for the convenience of building the interior. Then a longitudinal flat or angle bar around 1/4 inch by 1 1/2 inches by as long as you can handle is let into notches in the frames and wrapped around the hull. These "longs," spaced about 12 to 14 inches, are very lightly tacked to the frames.

■ **Steel hull Diesel
Duck 38, metal
work completed,
is waiting for
sandblasting
and paint. Photo
courtesy of Custom
Steel Boats,
Merritt, North
Carolina.**

Next, the plate is hung. Using two plates per side and two per bottom, each plate is welded to an end then wrapped around the hull. You then go inside the hull, and wherever the plate isn't touching a long you release the weld holding the long to the frame and, by using heat, let the long flow out to touch the plate. Then you weld the longitudinals to the plate. The plate is never welded to a frame. The resulting hull is so smooth and fair that it's next to impossible to tell the difference between steel and plywood without banging on it.

Any hull design can be built by this method, but single-chine design is by far the simplest and quickest to build and so is the most common. Multichine construction is common with sailing hulls, but this adds another whole plane to the structure and is more trouble than it's worth. Steel doesn't like to bend several directions at once, and plating up a round-bilge hull with reverse curves requires a good deal of skill and ideally the use of a plate-bending machine. I have seen round-bilge steel hulls "planked up" lapstrake fashion from spiled steel planks, 10 inches wide or less. This really looked sharp, but just thinking about the amount of plate cutting and welding involved makes me tired.

As mentioned earlier, steel is so strong that many designers look just at the material's theoretical strength and specify plating as thin as 1/8 inch supported by an elaborate frame. This is a mistake, in my opinion. The thin plating wants to wrinkle when you're welding it onto the hull, it's puncture prone, and it flexes enough underway to make the boat sound like the inside of an oil drum. I wouldn't use anything thinner than 3/16-inch plate on the hull or deck; this can be supported by a heavy, simple structure rather than one made up of many little pieces, and you get a hull rugged enough to absorb considerable abuse. The thick plating won't rust or get eaten away by electrolysis before you notice the problem and can deal with it, and it is thick enough so that it *wants* to wrap smoothly onto the hull. If the displacement of the boat you're planning won't handle at least 3/16-inch plate, you'd be better off using plywood.

Steel hulls suffer from condensation as badly as fiberglass and so need to be insulated. Traditionally, a spray-applied foam completely covers the inside structure. This stops condensation, but the foam is flammable so you need to be sure you're through welding before using it. It's a good idea to bolt on wood strips to carry the wood interior, spaced about 1/2 inch from the steel frames and deck beams so the foam covers the steel completely. If you don't, as my friend Charlie didn't with the incredible round-bilge reverse-curve sailboat he built, in cold weather the exposed tips of the deck beams condense water and drip it on you.

Untreated steel can rust away as much as 1/16 inch a year, but today's epoxy-based coatings have solved this problem and steel is now very low maintenance. Electrolysis can still kill you, though. If you get a battery lead in bilgewater or tie up in a marina where some idiot lets his power cord dangle in the bay, you can have big trouble fast. This is easily avoided by using sacrificial zinc plates, however, and there are many very old steel boats around testifying to the material's longevity.

Steel is a good material for backyard boatbuilders, but here's what I dislike about it: it's cold, heavy, dirty, and noisy to work with. It must be sandblasted and coated with chemicals if it is to last. It must be heavily insulated inside down to the waterline (as do fiberglass and aluminum and cement—everything except wood) with spray-applied foam.

But the advantages of steel far outweigh its disadvantages. Steel may be no fun to work with, but at least the necessary skills are easily acquired and the tools are few and inexpensive; about $1,000 will get you everything you need. Lots of folks take a community college night class and emerge six months later with the skill to build their own boat or even take a welding job. There's no way you can learn woodworking anywhere near that quickly, and the schools around the country who claim otherwise are conning you.

Lots of folks know how to weld, and hiring good help at a reasonable rate is easy. If you don't want to build your own boat, the next least expensive way is to serve as your own contractor and hire the help. I'd still learn the basics of welding, just so you can tell if your help is doing it right. And finding a yard to build a steel boat is easy; they're all over the place.

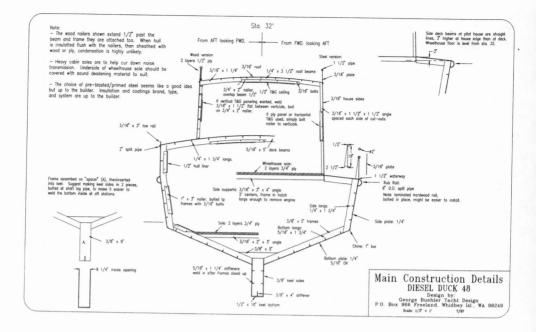

Sta. 32'

From AFT looking FWD. — — From FWD. looking AFT

Note:
— The wood nailers shown extend 1/2" past the beam and frame they are attached too. When hull is insulatted flush with the nailers, then sheathed with wood or ply, condensation is highly unlikely.

— Heavy cabin soles are to help cut down noise transmission. Underside of wheelhouse sole should be covered with sound deadening material to suit.

— The choice of pre-blasted/primed steel seems like a good idea but up to the builder. Insulation and coatings brand, type, and system are up to the builder.

Wood version
2 layers 1/2" ply
3/16" x 1 1/4"
3/16" roof
1/4" x 3 1/2" roof beams
Steel version:
1 1/2" pipe
3/16" plate

3/4" x 2" nailer, 1/2" T&G ceiling 3/16" bolts
overlap beam 1/2"
If vertical T&G paneling wanted, weld 3/16" x 1 1/2" flat between verticals, bolt on 3/4" x 2" nailer.
If ply panel or horizontal T&G used, simply bolt nailer to verticals.
3/16" house sides
3/16" x 1 1/2" x 1 1/2" angle spaced each side of cut-outs.

Side deck beams at pilot house are straight lines, 3" higher at house edge than at deck. Wheelhouse floor is level from sta. 32.

3/16" x 3" toe rail
2" split pipe
1/4" x 1 3/4" longs.
1/2" hull liner
5/16" x 5" deck beams
Wheelhouse sole:
2 layers 3/4" ply
1/2"
2 1/2"
2 1/2"
18"
3/16" plate
1 1/2" waterway
Rub Rail:
6" O.D. split pipe
Note: laminated hardwood rail, bolted in place, might be easier to install.

Frame assembed on "spacer" (A), then inserted into keel. Suggest making keel sides in 2 pieces, butted at shaft log pipe, to make it easier to weld the bottom inside at aft stations.

Sole supports: 3/16" x 3" x 4" angle 2" centers, frame in hatch large enough to remove engine.
1" x 3" nailer, bolted to frames with 3/16" bolts
Side longs:
1/4" x 1 3/4"

A. 3/8" x 9"
Sole: 2 layers 3/4" ply
3/8" x 5" frames
Bottom longs:
5/16" x 1 3/4"
Side plate: 1/4"
3/16" x 2" x 3" angle
3/8" x 5"
Chine: 1" bar

9 1/4" inside opening
5/16" x 1 1/4" stiffeners weld in after frames stood up
3/16" keel sides
3/8" x 4" stiffener
1/2" x 10" keel bottom
Bottom plate: 1/4"
5/16" OK

Main Construction Details
DIESEL DUCK 48
Design by:
George Buehler Yacht Design
P.O. Box 966 Freeland, Whidbey Isl., WA 98249
Scale: 1/2" = 1'   7/97

■ Steel construction Diesel Duck 48, cross-section view.

A steel hull of 3/16-inch or heavier plate is so strong that few things can damage it; a steel boat will bounce off reefs and swat away bullets. Steel doesn't rot, and the sun doesn't make it brittle as it does fiberglass. It is easily worked, and almost every small port in the world will have someone who can weld. In fact, many steel-boat owners carry small welders aboard so they can work on their own boats, or as is usually the case, earn money while cruising. It seems there's always room in a small community, especially in an expatriate boating community, for another welder.

Steel is cheap and easily available worldwide. For a good cost guesstimate, figure 50 to maybe 65 percent of the displacement (weight) of a steel hull will be the steel itself. The 48-foot Diesel Duck (Appendix I) has about 33,000 pounds of steel in her. New steel in 1998 America is about 30 cents a pound or less. Without figuring waste, she'd have about $10,000 worth of steel in her. And a steel boat is very quick to build. A good welder can throw together a large steel boat in just a few months, although of course finishing out and outfitting takes as much time as with any other boat. But a basic steel single-chine hull package, with decks and house, all sandblasted and barrier coated, can be built quite rapidly.

Materials costs for a wood hull vary with location. For example, good white oak is available and reasonable in New Jersey but terribly expensive in California. Looking at the 48-

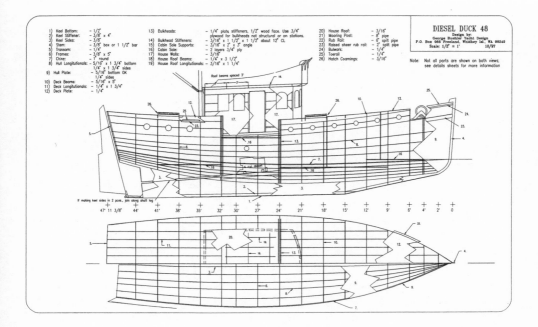

DIESEL DUCK 48
Design by:
George Buehler Yacht Design
P.O. Box 966 Freeland, Whidbey Isl., WA 98249
Scale: 1/2" = 1'   10/97

Note: Not all parts are shown on both views;
see details sheets for more information

■ Steel construction Diesel Duck 48, full construction plan.

foot Duck again, if she were built of construction-grade materials here in the Northwest, the materials costs would be very close to that of steel. Without factoring in waste, which might run 10 percent, her 1,407 square feet of 1/4-inch steel hull plate would cost about $4,305. With wood composite construction, using an inner layer of 3/4-inch fir topped with three layers of 3/8-inch plywood, the hull skin would be about $4,100 plus another $1,500 or so for fasteners and goops. If she were built in Mississippi of pressure-treated pine, she might be even less. The labor rate will be higher than for steel, of course, because the building time is considerably longer and a skilled wood boatbuilder is harder to find and charges more than a skilled welder. On top of that, the quality of the wood won't be first class, and the resale value will be less than if she were built of steel.

One of my clients tried to beat this by having a 72-footer built from solid teak in Malaysia. Yes, the materials costs were very low for top-quality wood, and the labor rates were low, too. But the workers' productivity was very low as well, and all the miscellaneous parts, the bolts and screws and glues and so on, cost several times as much as in the States and were hard to find.

Wood is an excellent choice for a home builder because it's clean and easy to work, it isn't noisy and so won't bother the neighbors, and it can be purchased one small piece at a time. But unless you have a great deal of disposable cash, I don't think it's very feasible to hire the building of a larger wood boat. You can do much better for the money with steel.

Lately I've been thinking that it might be interesting to couple a heavily plated steel hull with a deck built of heavy laminated wood beams covered with plywood. That way you'd have the advantages of the steel hull with the warmth, looks, quiet interior, and all-round feel of a wood boat. The best way to do this seems to be to weld a heavy (something like 1/4-inch × 12-inch) flange clear around the inside of the sheer. You could hang the wood deck beams from the flange, then overlap it with the plywood deck, stopping about 2 inches from the sheer to provide a good waterway. You'd want to epoxy-coat the wood where it touches the steel and bed it very well in something sticky as hell. It's something to think about.

Some folks are interested in grades of steel that resist corrosion better than good old mild steel, but these alloys cost more, they're harder to work, and they're more brittle and so more susceptible to fatigue failure. Today's new protective coatings make them completely unnecessary. Old-time mild steel, welded with 6011 rod, is the best choice. It costs the least, both for materials and labor, has better fatigue resistance than any of the other varieties, and with minimal care will last longer than you will.

As steel boats have become more popular their resale value has climbed. Since the cheap material and fast building time (read low labor costs) will have you into the boat for less than any other material, you'll have more boat for the bucks; should you want to sell it someday, you'll be able to price it very attractively, compared with other boats, and still come out all right.

ALUMINUM

ALUMINUM CONSTRUCTION is becoming popular these days. The marine-grade aluminums are almost eternal, requiring no maintenance other than electrolysis prevention and of course antifouling bottom paint. You don't really need to paint the topsides, and unpainted aluminum boats are common, with the result that aluminum is generally considered the ultimate low-maintenance material.

Aluminum is easier to cut and shape than steel; you can saw it out with a common Skilsaw. Aluminum is very light for its strength and so is an ideal choice when weight is an issue, which is why many big sailboats and planing power yachts are built from it. But aluminum's downsides far outweigh its positives for boats like we're talking about, and I recommend against it for most uses for a number of reasons.

Aluminum is much more expensive than steel and is more complicated to weld, requiring more expensive welding gear as well as shielding from the weather. Steel welders seem to be all over the place, but good aluminum welders are harder to find, so the labor rates are higher if you're hiring the boat built.

Aluminum is terribly susceptible to electrolysis, and a stray current can kill an aluminum boat in no time. Admittedly this isn't a normal occurrence, but electrolysis presents more of a danger than it does with steel.

Since aluminum is quite light you'll need to ballast the hull heavily to bring it down to its marks. That's fine for a sailboat, but a high ballast ratio in a powerboat makes no sense, because the resulting low center of gravity will produce a boat with a terribly jerky motion at sea. I've heard of aluminum power cruisers with such a fast and jerky roll that lead weights had to be bolted to the pilothouse roof to raise the center of gravity and slow it down!

Given these negatives, I see no reason to spend the extra money on an aluminum boat. One man who priced out both steel and aluminum for a 40-footer told me that he could buy the steel *and* an engine for what the aluminum alone would have cost. The only way I could justify aluminum is if I really needed the light weight, say with something really long and narrow. Even then I'd think twice, given the added risk of electrolysis.

FIBERGLASS

FIBERGLASS IS PROBABLY the ideal material for a production boat. Once the molds are made, unskilled labor can turn out the hulls, decks, and interior "modules" in short order. But a custom fiberglass hull is a major deal, requiring far more labor than any other material. First you make a mold, then you fair the mold, then you lay up the hull, then you have to fair that. And you still don't have much, because the molded hull flexes all over the place, and plastics will fatigue and break under prolonged flexing. So before you can start building anything into the hull, you have to stiffen it by fitting in bulkheads and a sheer stringer. "Glassing" things to fiberglass is no fun; the reeking fiberglass fumes burn your eyes and leave you nauseated, and you will spend months breathing them before the fiberglass shell is to the point where you can start building anything into it.

Fiberglass is as condensation-prone as steel and so must be insulated. Fiberglass home builders frequently use wood decks and houses because they are much simpler to build than the fiberglass equivalent, which makes me think these folks should have used wood (or steel) for the hull, too. In addition to the stink, the hassle, and the eternal itching from all that fiberglass dust and the wear and tear on your lungs unless you dress up like a frogman, one-off fiberglass construction is the most expensive construction method, both for materials and time.

If you're really intent on a fiberglass boat, you might investigate a material called C-Flex, which consists of "planks" of fiberglass rods joined by fiberglass fabric. To construct a boat with this stuff, you set up wood stations just as with traditional bent-frame wood construction, staple the C-Flex planks onto that, then lay down layers of fiberglass cloth set in resin. I've seen this done several times and it's pretty slick. You'll still have a lot of laborious fairing to smooth the finished hull, but C-Flex does make fiberglass feasible for custom boatbuilding, it can be delivered by UPS if you live far from boatbuilding materials suppliers, and the basic work of building the hull is very low tech; as long as you keep the temperature within tolerances and stir the mix, the chemicals will work.

Fiberglass hulls have good resale value and need relatively little maintenance, although they require annual buffing and waxing or painting to look halfway decent, which makes them no lower maintenance than steel or one of the epoxy-wood methods. The biggest disadvantage is that, for other than minor repairs such as cracks or blistering, which can be fixed with epoxy putty and a little mat and cloth, fiberglass is very difficult and time-consuming to repair. This is a big deal if you're trying to fix a hole in your boat on a beach between tides. With wood or steel you could get it done in time. In addition, some of the new resins—which replaced the early super resins that were just too poisonous—tend to soak up water or goof up in other ways that are just becoming evident.

Attaching an interior solidly to a fiberglass hull can be a difficult task. In the 1980s a hurricane hit Cabo San Lucas, blowing a lot of boats up on shore. Many of the fiberglass hulls were completely destroyed, but the interesting thing was that many of their interiors completely separated from the hulls and ended up as scraps littering the beach.

Plastic boats do have a bad rep in some quarters, but this comes mostly from a few production companies that push the limits of how weak they can build a boat and still get someone to buy it. A heavy-duty fiberglass boat will work just fine. Still, I don't like them at all, for the reasons just listed and for emotional reasons as well. Yacht designer L. Francis Herreshoff compared fiberglass to "frozen snot," and said boats made of it were good only for "the sons of labor organizers to take Bad Girls up the river in." Yet fiberglass does have its place, and with C-Flex construction it's at least worth considering.

FERROCEMENT

FERROCEMENT AT LEAST needs to be mentioned. Most people dismiss it right off, and banks and insurance companies are very hesitant about it, so the resale value of a cement boat is usually zilch. The problem is that they are almost impossible to survey without X-ray equipment, and so many terrible ones were built that all of them suffer a bad reputation. This is the unfortunate result of a con man who in the 1960s set up ferrocement dealerships all over the country and advertised that people could build cement boats for a fraction of its true cost. Sure a 50-foot cement hull might cost only $3,000, but when you build a custom boat you quickly learn the hull is the least expensive part! These dealerships sold plans, rented out building sites, and of course sold all the hardware and outfitting gear. Thousands of people got sucked into this stuff, and while many boats were completed and some were even pretty decent, by the mid-1970s hundreds of abandoned cement hulls were lying around the country. I haven't seen a new one under construction in the United States for years, but I still occasionally see an abandoned cement hull out in a pasture, and recently I read where a Californian was going around and hauling them off for free, then converting them into septic tanks.

But if you can forget its history of abuse, there's a lot to be said for ferrocement. When properly built it's really strong stuff. It's dirt cheap, and the materials—mostly just a reinforcing bar framework covered with steel mesh that is then covered with plaster—are available anywhere. It requires little skill except in the plastering phase, and you can hire masons to help there. Like C-Flex, it's ideally suited for curved shapes, so you can reproduce a reverse-curved round-bilge hull easily with it.

Cement construction is going strong in Third World countries because, while the method is labor intensive, it's inexpensive, environmentally friendly, and requires such low skill. Cuba in particular has made an international name for itself for fine large cement fishing boats.

If you start building a new cement boat you'll get nothing but static from everybody, but there are times when it makes sense. For instance, I've always loved the West Coast halibut schooners, but building one from wood would be impossible today; the materials alone would cost a fortune, and even assuming you could find the skilled labor necessary to do it, this would cost even more. But in ferrocement, a halibut schooner becomes feasible.

The big threat to cement hulls is electrolysis, and any through-hull or rudder fitting must be completely isolated from the cement hull's steel "armature." This requires careful layup and lots of preplanning;

if electrolysis does get into the armature you're dead. I've seen cement hulls that were in places just scales, with no steel left inside. There's no way to fix that.

Cement suffers from the same condensation problems as steel and plastic unless it's insulated, and attaching an interior is also really difficult. The simplest system is to plan flanges in the armature layup, bolt heavy plywood bulkheads to those, then hang the interior from that. And if I were building one I think I'd add a good layer of epoxy and cloth on the outside just as a watertight backup.

One of the finest cruising boats I've ever seen was built by the American Concrete Institute to show what a ferrocement boat could be. My friend Dick Marsh sailed it to the Tropics and back, even going through a hurricane without problems.

Resale value I've mentioned before, and I suppose we need to look at that a little more closely. I never worry about "resale," because doing so means you'll end up with something that isn't exactly what you want. Of course a home-built label hurts resale right off, and this has always infuriated me because many homebuilts are better built than lots of commercially built boats, especially when you throw production boats into the equation. Herreshoff, Atkin, Bill Garden, and some other top designers also built boats, and to have theirs or your work put down because it doesn't say "Bayliner" on the side is really dumb. But banks can look up a production boat in the Blue Book and see the market value, and a custom boat is confusing to many of them.

Fortunately not all banks are that ignorant, and if you first find a surveyor who actually knows what he's talking about, many banks and insurance companies will take his word for it. Dealing with cash customers is easier! When I sell a "homemade" boat, I say "Damned right it's homemade! I ain't going offshore in something I didn't oversee the construction of myself! This here is one quality-built boat!"

Regardless of the quality of the design or the quality of the boat, however, in reality the only professionally built custom boats that sell for close to their original cost are those from one of the big-name yacht firms. That's an unfortunate fact of life and makes little sense. On top of that, our Troller Yacht is a unique craft, especially with the interior set up for your personal tastes. When you go to sell it, you'll see boats that aren't anywhere near as safe and solid going for more than you can get, because yours is different from what the public sees in the boating magazines. Regardless of the construction material, it won't sell right off, and probably won't sell for what you think it's worth unless you wait long enough for a person who understands what it is to come along.

That's why I never worry about resale. No boat is an investment, and if you worry about that stuff you'll never have any fun. Build what you want, to do what you want done. A very wealthy friend of mine has no fun at all. All he does is work to make more money. But you know, a bank statement, regardless of the number of zeros on it, is pretty useless by itself. It doesn't even make decent toilet paper!

Systems

THIS BOOK IS ABOUT practical long-range cruising boats, "practical" being defined as affordable by the average working person and reliable enough to venture out to sea without worrying you'll get stuck somewhere you don't want to be. Central to both affordability and reliability are a boat's systems.

The systems on our Troller Yacht differ little from those on a long-range cruising sailboat, except that a Troller Yacht needs to carry more fuel and will likely have multiple tanks hooked together in some way. The sail rig will be simpler, and we'll likely have two steering stations. But all the other systems for common tasks like anchoring, cooking, and sanitary needs are essentially the same for power or sail.

Numerous books discuss specific systems and how to install them, so I won't go into that here. (See Appendix IV for a recommended reading list. In general, I prefer books written before 1980, because those authors were a little more down to earth about things.) Instead, I'll concentrate on the *concept* of systems that work on long-range cruising powerboats, because—believe me—it's easy to get carried away with this if you're at all susceptible to advertising.

There's something about powerboats that makes people want to load them down with exotic systems. Whenever the main engine is shut down, their big diesel generators must run to power the electric cooking and pressure-water systems, the air conditioning and VCRs and television and freezers and everything else associated with a shoreside home. Of course many larger new sailboats are also outfitted in this fashion, and there's nothing wrong with doing things like this if that's what you want. But these systems are expensive and the maintenance will become overwhelming, requiring the frequent (and expensive) attention of skilled technicians to keep everything operational.

For serious open-water cruising, outfitting a boat as though it were a big motor home or a small house will cause you major problems and can even be dangerous. The problem is the marine environment. Salt air gets into everything, and electrical systems in particular just don't live long around salt water. The only advantage to all these elaborate systems is that if you know how to repair them, you can make big money fixing all the yachts broken down in cruising ports around the world.

As I mentioned earlier, I'm not advocating going cruising on the cheap. Quite the contrary. While it's true that an all-round low-tech approach makes a boat considerably less expensive than a typical production trawler, I advocate the low-tech path less for low initial cost than for long-term reliability. I want the very best systems on my boat: a top-quality engine, heavy-duty anchoring and steering systems, redundant fuel filtering and transfer systems, top-quality galley gear, and so on, all installed so that everything is fully accessible for easy maintenance. These are all crucial for successful long-range cruising.

If your boat will be used only for coastal cruising, or if you'll be living aboard in a marina (as most people do), there's no reason not to install whatever systems you feel will make the boat more homelike. If something important fails, you'll never be too far from parts and competent service. I'm not criticizing that approach; just reminding you that this stuff is simply not going to work day in and day out in the rigors of ocean cruising without eventually bringing major headaches. And I especially want to remind you that none of these elaborate systems is actually necessary, no matter what the ads say.

At the 1996 West Marine Trawlerfest, I was one of three designers answering questions from people sufficiently interested in cruising powerboats to actually pay to hear us. Practically the whole session ended up being about outfitting. We talked about electric versus propane, preventing roll, sizing generating plants, methods of backup propulsion, and so on. Toward the end of the discussion I finally said—and it needed to be said: "I think a lot of you folks should reexamine what you want to do, because frankly, it sounds like you'll be happier with a motor home." For some reason I'm rarely invited back to these things.

So with your Troller Yacht, think simple, and if you're of a traditional mind—and I admit to suffering from a tinge of this—think traditional, too. These boats have a wonderfully traditional history behind them and are every bit as "shippy" as traditional sailboats. If you want to wear a Turkish fisherman's cap, get an earring, and add "Arrrrrrr" to your vocabulary, don't let the presence of an engine stop you. Troller Yachts reek of seamanship, individualism, and all-round Manly Men and Strong Competent Women stuff just as much as the most macho gaff-rigged schooner and far more so than the typical plastic sailboat. If you want to use kerosene cabin lights, navigate with a sextant, and outfit your Troller Yacht like a Tahiti Ketch, go for it.

ELECTRICITY

AS I'VE SAID MORE THAN ONCE, depending on anything electrical is risky on a boat because salt air raises hell with electrical stuff. But I've lived aboard three boats that had only kerosene lights, and I'm tired of not being able to read in bed. My current boat has a basic electric lighting system, but it also has kerosene lamps because I like them, use them regularly, and should the electric system goof up, I'll still have cabin lighting, even though I won't be able to read in bed.

So how much electricity do you need? The answer is, it depends. When you're traveling, a high-output alternator on the engine puts out plenty of juice. The problem comes when you're at anchor. How dependent on electricity do you want to be?

You always need to have enough battery power to start the engine, and this needs to be kept separate from anything else. Since I'm advocating a minimum dependence on electricity, four heavy-duty 12-volts installed in two separate banks, with two batteries wired in parallel in each bank, will be more than enough for the average cruising boat. A battery switch keeps each side isolated. At anchor you run off one side, keeping the other side, or perhaps a third separate battery, fully charged for starting the engine. When running, you switch them together so that both sides stay fully charged. Even then it's wise to keep one fully charged battery out of the loop if you're running anything electrical underway.

I learned this the hard way. We were running all night on an autopilot, and I didn't notice that the alternator belt was slipping. When the belt finally gave, the engine started overheating. I shut it down and fixed the belt, then found the batteries were too low to restart the engine. This was a stupid accident that wouldn't have happened if we had kept one battery always charged. You can buy automatic battery switching devices, but I prefer to do it manually, since I want only myself to blame in the event of failure.

When at anchor, there are a number of ways to keep the batteries topped up. Solar power panels are now so compact and inexpensive that it's sensible to install one or two on the roof, providing a constant trickle charge to the battery bank. Some cruisers use wind generators, which provide more output than a reasonably sized bank of solar panels (albeit for about the same money). I prefer the quiet rumble of a well-muffled diesel to the constant whoosh-whoosh and rattle of a wind generator, and if I were anchored somewhere in a nice, quiet cove and somebody came in with one of those, I'd probably end up shoving a dinghy oar into its blades.

Diesel-powered gensets have become so compact and reliable (and not *too* terribly expensive: a 4-kW diesel system currently costs around $5,000) that installing one can be very tempting if you have the room. Were I thinking about one of these, I'd probably be tempted to go further and get one big enough to bolt on a chain sprocket that could turn the propeller shaft should the propulsion engine fail. But now you're getting up into the price range of the main engine itself, and since I avoid electrical-powered primary systems for reliability reasons, I'd end up paying for a lot of electrical output I don't need. After all, the Troller Yacht has sail as a backup system, and this is so reliable that a backup engine is superfluous. And maintaining a whole second engine doesn't interest me in the least. Did you catch that? It isn't the *cost* of the genset that changes my mind; it's the maintenance.

But what if you want to run electric tools? There's two ways: You can install an *inverter* that changes 12-volt direct current to the 110-volt alternating current necessary to run most power tools. A marine-grade inverter that handles 1,400 watts, enough to run a desktop computer or most small tools, will cost you about $500. You can wire this into the system and have several 110-VAC outlets placed strategically around the boat. When you need household current, just switch on the inverter—although it's a good idea to do this when the main engine is running, because these things suck juice big time.

I went for an even simpler system, however: a 2.5-kW generator powered by a rope-start gas lawnmower engine. It's lightweight, costs less than 400 bucks, and is very reliable although noisy as hell. But it's all I need on those few occasions I have to run an electric tool like a saw or drill or sander, and in the highly unlikely event my batteries all go flat, it will charge them up. It stores easily in a deck locker and might get used three times a year. Most of us carry a few gallons of gas for an outboard, so carrying another 3 gallons (translating to six hours running time for the generator) isn't a problem. In fact, the little genset's Briggs & Stratton engine runs okay on oil-mixed outboard gas. This thing is really handy if you're careened on a beach somewhere for painting or minor repairs and there's no shore power. It's light enough to take to shore if you want to work on larger projects, say sanding and painting the skiff, without messing up the boat.

Most other appliances, except for tools, are available in 12-volt versions, so you shouldn't need more 110 than a little portable genset can provide. I do quite a lot of writing on the boat, for instance, but I use a notebook computer plugged into a 12-volt cigarette-lighter receptacle mounted by the desk. If you want to use a large monitor you'll need 110, but you'll probably conclude the small screen is a lot less hassle.

WATER

HOW MUCH WATER DO YOU NEED? One-half gallon a day per person used to be considered a comfortable ration for cruising sailboats, figuring dishwashing with seawater and not showering between ports. That doesn't sound like much water, but I've lived with those limitations for as long as 40 days and it's no problem at all. I'd bathe regularly in seawater, since it doesn't bother my skin, and rinse my hair with fresh water. More sensitive types will need a freshwater rinse to get the salt off.

When you're on passage, especially in a powerboat, your body uses very little energy and therefore needs less fuel and water; you're pretty much just sitting or laying down most of the time. Most powerboats have inside steering, so it's possible you'll never even go outdoors. Robert Beebe mentioned one Atlantic crossing during which he never even got out of his bedroom slippers! Your greatest energy drain will be the constant bracing or slight tensing of muscles as the boat rolls; this is almost an automatic reflex, and it takes time to learn to just go with the flow.

It's smart to maintain some rationing schedule, just on the off-chance that something keeps you at sea longer than you expected. We can easily carry 150 to 200 gallons of water in even small boats, so increasing the daily ration beyond a gallon a day is certainly possible. It's a good idea to keep track of what you use shoreside for a few days, then base your cruising ration on that. You'll be surprised to discover how little water you actually use.

It's also a good idea to divide your capacity among a series of smaller tanks, say 25 gallons each, rather than to use one or two big tanks. As long as you install shutoff valves in each line, keeping the tank closed off until you actually need to use it, you'll never have a major loss of water.

Many cruising sailboats carry just one or two 20-gallon tanks hooked to the sink faucet, and another 60 or 80 gallons in 5-gallon containers. There's several advantages to this and it's worth considering for our Troller Yacht.

Away from the United States, few places will have water at the

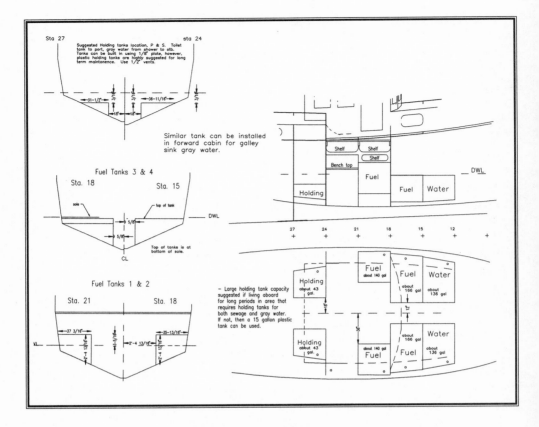

Sta 27   sta 24

Suggested Holding tanks location, P & S. Toilet
tank to port, gray water from shower to stb.
Tanks can be built in using 1/8" plate, however,
plastic holding tanks are highly suggested for long
term maintenence. Use 1/2" vents.

Similar tank can be installed
in forward cabin for galley
sink gray water.

Fuel Tanks 3 & 4
Sta. 18

Sta. 15

Fuel Tanks 1 & 2
Sta. 21   Sta. 18

– Large holding tank capacity
suggested if living aboard
for long periods in area that
requires holding tanks for
both sewage and gray water.
If not, then a 15 gallon plastic
tank can be used.

Shelf Shelf
    Shelf
Bench top
Fuel
Holding   Fuel Water DWL

Holding
about 43
gal. Fuel
about 140 gal Fuel Water
     about
     166 gal about
       136 gal

Holding
about 43
gal. about 140 gal about
Fuel 166 gal Water
  Fuel Fuel about 136 gal

■ Water and fuel tank layout. Note that these steel tanks built into a steel hull are located to keep weight more or less even on each side of CB so that the boat will maintain its trim regardless of tank level. Fully loaded fuel and water tanks will weigh several tons and can effect a smaller boat's trim.

dock and very little of this will be drinkable. Since you'll often need to lug water to the boat, it makes sense to store it in the carrying containers. Two 5-gallon jugs are the largest you can conveniently carry very far, and 3-gallon jugs are easier. With water stored all over the boat in small jugs, you'll never have a total system failure, you'll have additional storage space without bilge-robbing built-in tanks, and the jugs are far less expensive than large custom-built tanks. Your main water tank can be heavy plastic bought to fit an existing space (check marine supply catalogs for dimensions).

This system makes even more sense if you have a watermaker; these have become so cheap and reliable that installing one makes sense. One on the market ($1,550 retail in 1998) makes 1.4 gallons an hour, runs on 12 volts (so you don't need a 110 system), and can even be hand-operated if your electric system burns up; this makes it usable even in emergency situations. Add to the watermaker at least 30 gallons in small containers and one or two 20-gallon tanks, and the price is less than having large custom tanks built in, and to me at least is way preferable. With a watermaker you can shower as much as you want, although I'd always keep a backup supply of water, say 30 days worth, on hand. You just never know.

Pressure-water systems are very convenient, but when I was cruising in sailboats I'd always disconnect the sink pump and fill a gallon jug each day so I could strictly ration water use. It's just too easy to use water if all you have to do is turn the faucet handle.

What do you do if the pressure-water system that runs the shower and sink faucets quits? Well, it's only sensible to install a backup hand pump at the sink, plumbed in to the main tanks. I even install a sea-water pump at the galley, on the off-chance that I'm somewhere with water clean enough to wash with and I was too cheap to buy a water-maker (or it's on the fritz).

To avoid the cost and maintenance of a pressure-water system, I'd rather let gravity deliver water. A simple gravity system consists of a small tank on the roof holding a day or so's water ration, filled by a pump from the main tanks. Five- or 7-gallon stainless beer kegs work well for this and add a rather shippy touch to the boat. You could install one over the galley sink and one over the head for the shower and hand basin; if you want some free solar preheating, you can paint them black.

The system I like best is to build-in house faucets, an in-line water heater (more on this later), and a scattering of 110-volt outlets wired as a separate system. This way, when you're at a marina, just hook your hose to the dock water and you'll have pressure water, then hook your power into the shore-power box and you'll have electrical outlets to power whatever you want. This whole system is completely separate from the boat's primary systems, and is very simple and inexpensive. Of course the downside is that once you get away from big cities, or even North America, you'll rarely find a place where you can "hook up," as the RV crowd say. But this dual system definitely makes a boat more convenient when living aboard in an American marina, without compromising its integrity as a reliable long-range cruising boat.

FUEL

THERE ARE TOO MANY VARIABLES to determine exactly how much fuel you need to carry. It all depends on the your boat's fuel consumption, how much range you want, and how much reserve you need to feel comfortable. In earlier chapters I've shown how fuel consumption and speed are related, and how, after you pass a speed equal to 1.15 times hull speed, fuel use increases far more rapidly than speed. If you want to cross the Atlantic, you need less fuel than if you're headed nonstop to Tahiti, but the speed you plan to travel makes a major difference in your range.

Here's some figures for a boat with a 40-foot waterline and 38,000 pounds displacement carrying 800 gallons of fuel, based on calm conditions or running with the weather. I've shown similar tables before, but the way fuel use increases with speed is so dramatic that it doesn't hurt to be reminded.

Running a 60- to 80-horsepower engine at 12 horsepower for long periods will probably load it up (which is why I recommend smaller engines than you usually see; you'll run them efficiently far more often than they'll slow you down), so let's use the 16-horsepower figures as a base. Running at a V/L of 1.2 is 7.59 knots for almost a 6,000-mile range, or 1.54 times more range than if you run at 8.22 knots (V/L of 1.3). If your trip is 2,500 miles, at 7.59 knots it'll take 13 3/4 days and you'll need 336 gallons of fuel. Running at 8.22 knots, you'll burn 517 gallons and cut trip time to 12 1/2 days. While both leave a good fuel reserve, speeding up means you're burning 181 gallons of fuel to save

V/L	Speed (knots)	Hp	Fuel/Hr (gal)	Range on 800 gallons (miles)
1.15	7.27	12	0.72	8,077
1.20	7.59	16	1.02	5,953
1.3	8.22	28.4	1.7	3,859
1.35	8.54	52.2	3.13	2,181

18 hours, and you'll probably have to live with more engine noise, since it's running harder.

It all depends on what you want to do, but if you're coming from a sailing background, keep in mind how happy you were to average 4 knots for even a week. To an old sailor, an effortless 7.59 knots day after day sounds like a fantasy! And notice that 800 gallons isn't enough to get there if you run at 8.54 knots. Speed costs! Of course our Troller Yacht can always sail the remaining distance if we run out of fuel, but I'd rather plan to match speed and fuel capacity for the longest trip I'm planning.

The weight of the fuel and room for the tanks is a consideration in smaller boats. It's a good idea to locate the tanks somewhere around the buoyancy center so that the boat's basic trim stays the same as fuel is consumed. If space is a real issue, I'd center the fuel weight a bit forward of the buoyancy center so that when fully fueled, the boat trims slightly bow down. The hull runs through the water easier that way, and as you use fuel it will trim back to the DWL.

I much prefer a series of smaller tanks rather than one or two big tanks, because there's less chance of a major fuel loss. Each tank can be plumbed separately, and the ones not in use can be shut off. This requires some attention to fuel used, but that isn't so difficult. You can install a fuel flow meter by the helm, a sight gauge on the tanks, or a normal automobile-style gauge. Or use a dipstick; that's the simplest! The fuel flow meter is cheap and quite handy for balancing fuel-to-speed use; you can see the fuel usage change as RPMs change. If you get one with an equalizer, it will serve as a fuel gauge as well.

Current U.S. Coast Guard regulations and insurance requirements say that fuel lines should exit tanks from the top. With traditional tanks, the line always exited from the bottom, with a shutoff valve at the tank. A small drain valve mounted into a pint-capacity "bubble" was welded to the bottom of the tank; because fuel floats on top of water, you could use this to drain off a pint of fuel once in a while and get rid of any water in the fuel. But because a few idiots wouldn't fix a bad valve leaking gasoline (*not* diesel) into their bilges and got culled from the gene pool, the law now says no lines can exit from the bottom. Well, top-draining tanks require a fuel pump, and these are potentially more dangerous than a bottom drain! If the fuel line separates, all the fuel can siphon from the tank. You're supposed to install antisiphon valves in the line at the top of the tank to prevent this. If you do follow the law and install a top "exhaust line" (as the line to the engine is called), I'd still install a bottom tank cup and drain. This will come in handy should you take on a load of bad Third World fuel; besides—and not that I'm advocating lawlessness here—you only run into really rigid Coast Guard inspections if you plan to charter the boat.

Diesel tanks are usually made from mild steel, although stainless, aluminum, and even epoxy-coated plywood are also seen. Mild steel tanks are the best choice. They're cheap to have made and will last forever, as long as the outside is painted with a good protective paint; diesel fuel will prevent the inside from rusting. I've seen some people use 30- or 50-gallon barrels for tanks. This works, but the metal is pretty thin and so must be well coated with a protective paint; if you're smart you'll install them so they can be easily replaced when they rust through.

Don't use tanks with inside galvanizing; this is common in older gas boats and, with gasoline, lasts forever. But diesel eats galvanizing, and when that happens your filters will clog up. Aluminum tanks are common on smaller production boats, but they're prone to sudden leakage, and I wouldn't use them. There's no reason at all to use stainless diesel tanks. Mild steel works just as well and costs far less.

The Gougeon Brothers (the WEST Epoxy people) publish literature on making diesel tanks of plywood heavily coated with epoxy. This would be an easy and inexpensive way to custom-build tanks into wood or glass hulls. I like the idea and think it has real possibilities, but I would never completely trust it, so if I were to try it I'd use a series of small tanks, probably no bigger than 50 gallons each.

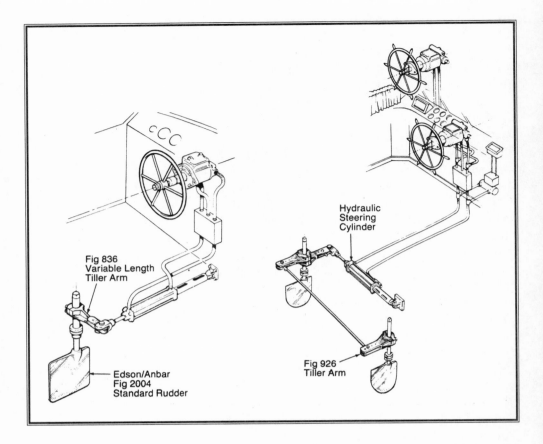

Fig 836
Variable Length
Tiller Arm

Hydraulic
Steering
Cylinder

Edson/Anbar
Fig 2004
Standard Rudder

Fig 926
Tiller Arm

■ Hydraulic steering installation. Edson Corporation of New Bedford, Massachusetts, makes all the parts necessary for any form of steering you want to install. It also makes top-quality bilge pumps, and various other accessories. This drawing is from Edson's excellent catalog.

Installing tanks in steel hulls is simple; just weld the sides and a top into the hull wherever you want a tank; the boat's hull serves as the tank bottom. Some folks also weld in a bottom, producing an entirely separate tank welded to the outside of the frames and giving the boat a "double hull" in the tank areas, which certainly doesn't hurt anything and can prevent your coating a coral reef with fuel oil if your attention span wanders and you run aground.

Tanks (fuel or water) of any size need inside baffles to keep the liquid from sloshing around. Aside from producing a constantly annoying sound, sloshing can lead to failure of anything but a welded steel tank.

And last, you want your fuel system equipped with good filtering and water-separating systems. Use a double filter system, with the fuel line plumbed so that you can route fuel to either filter; this allows you to change a filter while the engine is running, which avoids your having to bleed air from the system.

STEERING

THE STEERING SYSTEM is just as important as the propulsion system. It must be completely reliable, with all components readily accessible. A basic cable system wrapped around a steering-wheel-mounted drum is the least expensive way to go, very reliable, and completely "fixable" shipboard without special tools or parts. Use heavy wire rope running through large sheave blocks, and install everything so you can inspect the entire length and change the wire should you need to (expect 20 years minimum service).

Homemade mechanical steering systems used to be common. These use an automotive steering box to turn 3/4-inch pipe, with universal joints (usually from an automotive drive shaft) installed every place the shaft needs to bend on its way back to the rudder. This system has many advantages. It's direct, with none of the slack that can develop with a cable system. It's very rugged; who ever heard of a car's steering box failing? And it's very inexpensive; all the parts are available in any big-city wrecking yard. It's more trouble to install than a cable system and requires a little maintenance—you'll have to keep the universals greased—but it's just about foolproof.

■ A "fisherman style" two-station steering hookup. This owner is strictly concerned with function, not appearance. It is, however, a very inexpensive system, and is certainly easily maintained! Note the heavy-duty welded pipe railing on deck.

Both of these systems are easy to hook up with a second steering station, although it's easier if the station is directly over the main wheel, such as in a fly bridge. You'd simply bolt a chain sprocket to the main wheel's shaft, then run steering chain, or cable attached to chain, through the roof to a sprocket bolted to the second wheel. Be sure to use nonferrous material for all this or you'll never be able to adjust your compass.

As well proven and inexpensive as these systems are, however, there's a lot to be said for hydraulic steering. It's very reliable, although not necessarily cheap: an off-the-rack system can cost several thousand bucks to install. But if you really understand hydraulics, you can put together a system quite inexpensively from parts available in any industrial supply catalog. I suggest going with the marine systems only because the big-name companies like Wagner really make great stuff and you'll have no problems.

Hydraulic steering is very simple. A pump, attached to the steering wheel, is connected to a "ram" at the rudder by flexible hose, which makes the system very easy to install since the hose can be wrapped around obstacles. When you turn the wheel you pump hydraulic fluid through the hose, and the fluid pushes or pulls the ram, turning the rudder. These systems work with low pressure, and failure of any of the parts is practically unheard of. You can run back-up lines from the wheel to the ram if you're especially nervous about a line failing, although I've never heard of this happening. After all, look at a bulldozer or a backhoe, with its hydraulically controlled blade or shovel. The worst problem their hydraulic systems normally encounter comes from tearing off a hose in the brush. The pumps rarely fail, despite far greater strains and pressures than our little steering system ever sees. Hydraulics are the simplest way to mount a second steering station, since the hoses can easily be run anywhere you want. And all modern autopilots are designed to work with hydraulic steering systems.

No matter what type of steering system you use to turn the rudder, it is essential that the rudder post run up to the deck, or at least to just below the deck, with a small hatch (such as a large pipe cap) over it so that you can quickly attach an emergency tiller and steer manually should the need arise. A few years ago I was on a newly launched custom boat, and the hydraulic steering hadn't been properly bled. We got into the middle of the marina and the steering froze. Here we were, 23 tons of steel heading toward a $250,000 plastic sailboat. The owner immediately opened a valve that drained the hydraulic oil, relieving the pressure. He tossed me an 18-inch crescent wrench, which I hooked to the rudder post. Charlie worked the engine controls while I steered us into a slip, to the glass sailboat owner's immense relief.

INTERIOR SYSTEMS

ONCE IT'S STARTED, a diesel needs no electricity to run. This being the case, it seems really dumb to have your other important systems completely dependent on electricity. For me at least this rules out electric shifting (now seen on some pleasure boats), an electric anchor winch, and 100 percent electric lighting and water delivery. For water removal I'll want one or two 12-volt bilge pumps, since they're so easy to install and are maintenance-free until the day they die. But I always want a belt-driven main bilge pump hooked up to a Y valve, so that it can be rigged to pump out the boat in the event of a major problem or be switched over to pump seawater up to a deck hose.

But most of all, I want nothing to do with electric cooking.

As far as I'm concerned, a convenient galley is one of a long-range

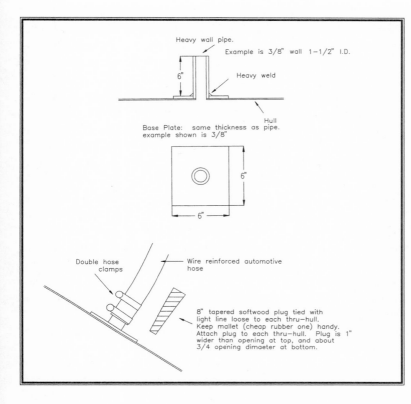

Heavy wall pipe.

Example is 3/8" wall 1–1/2" I.D.

6"

Heavy weld

Hull

Base Plate: same thickness as pipe.
example shown is 3/8"

6"

6"

Double hose
clamps

Wire reinforced automotive
hose

8" tapered softwood plug tied with
light line loose to each thru–hull.
Keep mallet (cheap rubber one) handy.
Attach plug to each thru–hull. Plug is 1"
wider than opening at top, and about
3/4 opening dimaeter at bottom.

■ This simple through-hull system is inexpensive and foolproof. It will not cause electrolysis, nor does it rely on any form of mechanical shutoff valve. Heavy-duty wire-reinforced radiator hose is very unlikely to fail, but if a problem does occur, the hose can be pulled and the plug driven in very rapidly. This idea is especially suited to steel boats, but the same system, bolted rather than welded down, can be used on wood or glass hulls.

cruising boat's top interior design requirements. Even the word "galley" implies something less than a real work-in kitchen, but this shouldn't be the case. You see, when cruising there's nothing to do except eat, so being able to provide good meals is important. I'm lucky enough to be married to a woman who thinks gourmet cooking is fun, and Gail's idea of a good time is the challenge of preparing five-star meals that don't also make you fat. And that requires a real kitchen.

Alcohol and kerosene are useless for real cooking stoves; they're fit only for weekending. Propane is the only sensible stove fuel unless you're spending most of your time in very cold weather. Then I'd probably use a diesel stove, because it will also heat the boat, but I'd still have a two-burner propane unit for warm weather, light meals, or for quickly boiling water.

Propane is readily available everywhere, and as long as you carry a variety of tank fittings you'll never have problems finding it. It's very cheap and efficient; 10 gallons of propane carried in two 5-gallon tanks will last months.

Propane does have a downside: It's quite explosive and heavier than air (and so sinks to the bottom, where it accumulates in the bilges, although it's hard to ignore that rotten-egg smell), and so must be installed very carefully. Still, this really isn't a problem. Just mount the tanks on deck or in a cockpit locker, so that any fuel leakage at the tank remains outside the hull. Install a pressure gauge in the line at the tank; if the system is tight, it should hold pressure for about 24 hours. If it doesn't, and if the leak is so tiny you can't smell the gas, you can find the leak by dabbing a bit of liquid dish soap on each connection until you find one that blows bubbles.

In a lifetime of messing with boats, I've probably seen most of the stupid and unlikely accidents that can happen, and I had an experience with propane that showed me just how hard it is to blow up your boat with it. One night I dropped in on a friend living aboard a sailboat. He had been drinking wine all evening, and I found him in the cabin holding a cigarette, with an electric heater sitting on the cabin sole and the boat absolutely reeking of propane. A stove burner had blown out and he hadn't noticed. I grabbed his cigarette and tossed it out the window, then dragged him outside and unplugged the shore-power line, since I was afraid of a spark if I turned off the heater with its switch. I don't remember how we got the gas out of the boat, although it seems to me we opened up everything and just let it air out. Since then I've respected propane but no longer fear it; if that boat didn't blow, it can't be that easy.

Propane stoves make your boat's kitchen as convenient as the one in your house. You can turn heat off and on immediately, broil steaks, and bake cakes. And since propane stoves are made by the millions, the stoves are inexpensive. Yes, you can spend $1,500 or more for a genuine marine stove made of stainless steel, but a top-grade propane range for a motor home costs about $400 and works exactly as well. Of course the RV stove isn't made from stainless and could start to rust in 10 years or so, but so what? Replace it!

Propane can be used for more than just cooking. In-line, "on-demand" hot-water heaters are easy to install and provide an endless supply of hot water. We've used a large in-line propane water heater in our house for 13 years and I'd never have anything else. Unlike a tank, it doesn't waste any space; it mounts on the wall above the clothes dryer. It's dirt cheap to operate because it only heats the water when you want hot water. The smaller units are so sensitive that they'll work with a boat's gravity-feed water system.

Propane refrigerators are common on boats. The burners don't work well unless they're sitting level—pretty hard to find at sea—so most people just turn them off between ports then fire them up at anchor and have all the ice cubes they can use. This isn't so bad. If you figure cruising along at a conservative 6 knots, that's 150 miles a day or 1,000 miles a week. Few passages will last much longer than two weeks, and living without a fridge for two weeks isn't a problem. I limit myself to two drinks a day at sea and can handle that without ice cubes. Fresh vegetables, fruits, eggs, butter, and so on keep well at sea. If you catch fish too big to eat in one day, you can cut it up for bait to use the next.

Twelve-volt fridges are very common, and the newer ones are quite efficient. These are easier to install than propane, don't consume cooking fuel, and can be used safely at sea. But at anchor, an electric fridge will require battery charging, meaning you'll have to run the main engine or have an auxiliary generator. Full-time refrigeration just isn't that high on my list of necessities. I think back to my sailboat days, and to me the idea of a fridge at anchor is most luxurious, and the simplest way to get this is with propane.

I saw one cruising boat that even had propane cabin lights. That's fine in cold climates, but it really heats up the cabin in the Tropics. If you actually want to heat up the cabin, propane furnaces and vented heaters are available. These work well for occasional use, but for serious heat a diesel heater is more efficient. Besides, it's easier to carry extra diesel than extra propane. But don't forget: Whenever you're traveling, an engine is running; right there is a great source of free heat, and it works just like the heater in your car. This simple, very reliable system channels engine cooling water through a small radiator, a fan blows air through the radiator, and the heat is ducted into the cabin. Although this is very common on commercial fishing boats, you rarely hear of it on pleasure boats, and I've never seen one on a production boat. I suppose it's too simple!

Automotive heater units are available in any car-parts catalog for under $200 or from a wrecking yard for a fraction of that. This idea works best with a "closed" freshwater cooling system, because the antifreeze in the system won't bother the heater core for years; when did you last replace your car's heater core? But the system will also work with seawater cooling, although you'll have to replace the radiator core from time to time.

On smaller boats, you can install the heater in the wheelhouse with the warm air directed around the rest of the boat with a common 12-volt fan. In larger boats, you could use a heavy-duty water pump to route cooling water to auto-type heaters mounted in several cabins. Be sure to install a solid gate valve in the heater hose line (both at the heater fixture and at the spot where the line branches off the main coolant line) so you can shut off the water in the event of a failure in the core or line. And it's a good idea to insulate the pipes between heaters and keep an eye on the engine's temperature gauge. An engine running too cool is headed for trouble (more on this below).

You won't see much in the marine press about using automotive and RV parts, but many things are available for cars and motor homes that work just as well on boats and cost considerably less than the officially approved marine version—propane ranges, pressure-water systems, 12-volt appliances, lighting fixtures, inverters, and tanks to name a few. You'll find tons of things you can use in a good automotive-parts catalog, such as J.C. Whitney's (available on most newsstands next to the hot-rod magazines), for good prices. For example, down at the marine store a year ago I paid $125 each for two heavy-duty windshield wipers with motors. They aren't even chrome. I just noticed heavy-duty wiper motors for off-road vehicles in the J.C. Whitney catalog for $27.

ANCHORING

ACRUISING BOAT NEEDS very good anchoring gear. What type of anchor you use is strictly a personal preference; there are many different designs and all have their believers and detractors, and all come equipped with a full complement of marketing hype. For instance, when you see an anchor demo at a boat show, bear in mind

that, at the 8:1 or 10:1 scope they use to tow their superanchor across a sandbox, almost any design will work, even a rock. One anchor on the market, which looks like a farmer's plow, is very popular and is reported to work quite well, but the great yacht designer L. Francis Herreshoff had this to say about it: "Mankind spent eons developing the most efficient shape to plow the earth, and what

■ **A self-storing hydraulic anchor winch aboard the troller *Frances* uses a short length of heavy chain connected to lighter-weight chain and no cable. Everything about this boat is first class.**

happened; some con man came along and started selling it as an anchor!" Since reading that, I've never been able to use one no matter how many cruisers say it's great.

About methods of lifting the anchor and storing the line I have no doubts, however: In my opinion the best system is a hydraulic self-storing cable winch. You rarely see these on yachts, but every West Coast fishing boat big enough for a winch has one bolted to its deck. There'll be a few hundred feet of galvanized wire cable attached to maybe 20 feet of heavy chain to provide weight to keep the anchor tending bottom, and then the anchor is attached to that.

This system has many advantages. It's very compact, cable being far less bulky than chain and thinner than the same strength rope;

everything stores on the winch drum, leaving the bow free for bosun's stores instead of being filled with heavy chain or bulky rope rodes (although I'd carry an extra nylon rode, just in case). Cable has much better abrasion resistance than nylon rope and is cheaper than rope and far cheaper than chain.

Heavy chain is better at providing a catenary cushion for the rode, but 20 feet of heavy chain added to the cable does keep the anchor on bottom; this is,

■ Braden Gearmatic Hydraulic Planetary Winch. While most trollers used homemade winches, Paccar Winch Divisions, in Broken Arrow, Oklahoma, makes a full line of winches. Photo courtesy of Paccar Winch Divisions.

after all, how most rope-based systems are configured. Cable also lacks the bungee-cord shock-dampening stretch of nylon (repeated shocks, as with an anchored boat being tossed by heavy seas, can break an anchor free), but in the rare event you need to anchor in an exposed place in the path of a hurricane, say, most systems will drag anyway; you'll have at least a fighting chance if you stay aboard and keep the engine running, using power to help maintain position.

Whether you use a self-storing winch (and I can't see why you wouldn't) or a normal yacht-style windlass, the best power source is hydraulic. It's bulkier than an electric winch, with an exposed hydraulic motor and hoses, but it's far less likely to fail. Besides, I rather like the rugged, shippy look. And once you've mounted the necessary hydraulic pump belt-driven from the main engine, you can run hydraulic hoses anywhere on the boat you want a winch. You might want one near the stern for pulling crab pots or on the mast for lifting the dinghy. Living on the boat for a while will give you many more ideas where you can put hydraulic power to work.

Only a few manufacturers in the United States make these winches, and they aren't cheap. But most winches on commercial boats are custom made, and any welding shop familiar with commercial boat work can make you one and design the hydraulic system; you can buy the basic pump, hoses, and valves through any industrial supply catalog. A walk down any commercial dock will show you dozens of these winches, and you can ask a boatowner who made his. Actually, in these days of diminished resources and increased regulations, you can ask the boatowner if he wants to *sell* his.

Several years ago I bought a small tractor with a homemade hydraulic bucket system, mostly to become more familiar with hydraulic systems, and I'm sold. This thing must have been 20 years old when I bought it, and in the years of clearing trails, carrying firewood, smoothing our road, and in general having fun avoiding work, I've never had any trouble. It hasn't leaked a drop of oil, blown a hose, or anything. The marine environment does present a problem with corrosion, so you should have your hoses made up with stainless fittings. You can protect the pump and motor itself by keeping them painted.

In the highly unlikely event that you suffer a hydraulic failure, winding the wire back in can be a big problem. If you're really cautious, you could have the winch built with a way to attach a handle to the axle; for example, welding a big nut to the axle end and carrying a 3/4-inch-drive socket wrench. Failing that, you can drag the cable aboard using a come-along; 1/8-inch line wrapped around the cable about 10 times will hold well enough to attach a come-along hook, as I found when the electric winch on a friend's boat goofed up.

I would never have an electric anchor winch on a boat. While they are more compact and customary equipment for the yachting crowd, eventually an electric motor—especially one exposed to the elements in a boat's bow—is going to burn out or be put out of operation by corroded wiring. I happened to be walking by a sailboat just as the wiring in its electric winch shorted out. Nobody was aboard, and the winch started trying to haul up the anchor, but it was up! The door was locked and I couldn't get aboard, so I just watched. Eventually the winch started smoking from the heat, and just about the time I had decided to kick in the door and pull a battery cable (I was worried a fire would start), the electric motor burned itself out. Granted, a situation like this is rare, but the more time you spend around boats the more rare situations you see. For instance, at this writing my friend Fred's 72-foot power cruiser is anchored near me with 150 feet of 1/2-inch chain out, and his electric anchor winch is burned out. After seeing (and experiencing) a lot of these rare situations, I'll only have systems on my boats that minimize the chances I'll suffer from one.

There's nothing wrong with manually operated winches; they're the least expensive and ultimately the most reliable. They're very common on sailboats and will work just as well on a powerboat. If someone slips the boat in and out of gear as you winch up, you'll keep the weight off the anchor until you get in all the scope. You can then use the engine to break the anchor free, making it easy to winch the thing up the rest of the way. This is a slow procedure, though, and to me it's far more appealing to leisurely touch a hydraulic lever and watch the anchor come up on its own.

Exhaust

BOTH "WET" (WATER-COOLED) AND "DRY" (just like your car) exhaust systems have their advocates, and both have pluses and minuses. Practically all sailboats and most power yachts have wet exhausts, where water is injected into the exhaust line to cool and muffle the gases and is discharged out the stern or the side somewhere near the waterline. The exhaust "pipe" can be heavy-wall wire-reinforced rubber hose, which is very easy to install, as you can wrap it around anything in its path. The cooling water, or *raw water,* as it's called, is pumped in from the ocean. If your engine is raw-water cooled, the exhaust water uses the same system; usually the engine-cooling water is simply ejected out the exhaust line. A *freshwater*-cooled engine will need raw water for a wet exhaust; this is supplied by a separate water pump that sucks the ocean up and into the exhaust line and a heat exchanger.

Wet systems have several advantages. They are relatively quiet and are much easier and often cheaper, at least initially, to install. The exhaust line remains cool enough not to burn you if you touch it, so it doesn't need to be insulated. The entire system takes up little space, and most of that is entirely below the sole or behind furniture. Because the exhaust exits near the waterline, you'll rarely get exhaust fumes in the boat unless you're running straight downwind.

On the downside, this is an entirely separate system that requires extra maintenance, and if, or rather when, parts fail, you're stuck without the right replacement. If the water flow stops, the exhaust hose will melt—and you may or may not smell it before it actually burns; I've melted one but not had a fire. Yet. The water flow will stop if the raw-water intake filter clogs, or if the raw-water pump belt or impeller (or both) wears out. I've had all three happen. The odds of a problem are greatly reduced if you replace all belts and impellers on a regular schedule, but I've even had a brand-new impeller fail, so carry several spares; the replacement parts are cheap and easy to store, so there's no excuse not to. I also suggest wiring a temperature alarm into the system. If you don't notice the engine starting to overheat, the alarm will alert you—assuming of course *it* doesn't fail! In a total failure of the heat exchanger or the raw-water pump, you can simply disconnect the freshwater system and hook it directly to the ocean. Pull the thermostat first, however; if you keep the seawater below 140°F it won't crystallize.

Most workboats have dry exhausts, and they are becoming more common in yachts. Dry exhausts are even more reliable than your car's system, because at sea you'll never jump a curb or a big rock and break things off.

A closed, freshwater engine-cooling system, where the engine cooling water, circulated by the engine's internal water pump, runs through a keel cooler (often just a long length of pipe) or heat exchanger outside the hull, is ideal for a dry exhaust and is used on almost every workboat from 30-foot Maine lobsterboats to 150-foot Alaska crabbers. A system like this is as simple and resistant to exhaust or cooling-system failure as can be, and the enclosed freshwater cooling system is practically maintenance-free. There's no reason why a raw-water cooling system won't work with a dry stack, but you'll need to install a water-straining filter system in the line, and this is a potential trouble spot. If you do install a strainer, and it's insane not to if you're relying on seawater for any part of your cooling system, mount it so the top of the line that brings water to the strainer is just above the waterline. This way you can disassemble the system to remove a plastic bag or a load of kelp and the boat won't fill with water. (Often it's easier to clear a clogged line by blowing air or water back through the intake than it is to pull through whatever's stuck, especially if something is partially clogging the through-hull inlet.)

With a dry-exhaust system, a pipe runs to a good muffler then up through the deck into a stack. The pipe needn't be perfectly straight, but any bends should be gradual; the harder it is for the gases to exit, the more power the engine wastes trying to get rid of them. The stack should be larger in diameter than the exhaust pipe (provide at least 6 inches of clearance all around the pipe), with vents on the side to admit cooling air. A dry-exhaust pipe will get very hot and so must be wrapped with pipe insulation wherever it is exposed or where someone could fall or accidentally lean against it.

Wet and dry systems both have their place. A dry exhaust has fewer parts and requires less maintenance; once it's installed you can essentially forget about it. Wet systems are easier to install, however, and sometimes are the only thing that will work. In most boats I prefer a dry system, especially if the engine is below the wheelhouse, because the dry stack is easily installed somewhere behind the house. For a boat without a real wheelhouse, for a real motorsailer, or if the engine is installed way back in the stern, a wet system is likely a better choice because there won't be a convenient place for a stack on deck.

ENGINE COOLING

YOU'LL USE RUBBER HOSES for most of the engine cooling and wet-exhaust systems, but you'll need metal couplings where hoses join. *Don't use stainless steel!* Stainless exhaust parts will look fine one day, show little "pimples" the next, and leak like a sieve soon after.

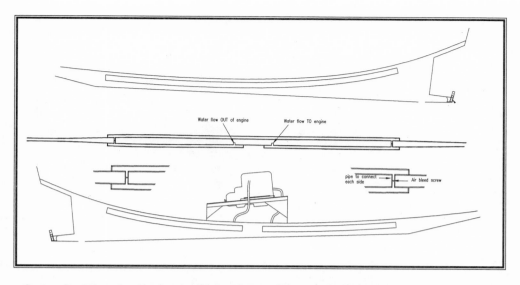

Water flow OUT of engine

Water flow TO engine

pipe to connect
each side

Air bleed screw

■ **Custom Steel Boats Inc. Freshwater Cooling System.** Heavy-wall split pipe is welded to each side of keel, connected by pipe through the keel at each end. Note the air-bleed port in each end pipe. Note also the water flow ports and the way the pipe is divided into two parts on one side of keel. The inside diameter (capacity) of the pipe depends on the horsepower and cooling requirements of the engine. This diagram shows a 72-horsepower diesel, 5-inch split pipe, installed on a Diesel Duck 38. According to Custom Steel Boats, this system works better than pipe laying on the inside bottom of the keel because it gets better cooling. Wood and fiberglass hulls can use a similar system, but the pipe will be whole rather than split, and will be attached to the hull with brackets.

Mild steel works better because it deteriorates evenly and obviously; all the connector parts can be made from common galvanized pipe. This is contrary to "common knowledge," but I learned it from the owner of a Seattle shop that builds cooling and exhaust systems for everything from little 10-horse sailboat auxiliaries to the massive diesels in oceangoing freighters. He said he tries to convince yachtsmen to avoid stainless because of the unpredictable way it deteriorates, but he's frequently ignored.

Be sure to carry a few extra pieces of pipe the same diameter as the inside of your cooling hoses and (if you have one) your wet-exhaust line. You'll want several straight 2-inch pieces and several 45- and 90-degree elbows, as well as a few extra feet of hose of each size and an assortment of hose clamps. If something overheats and melts part of a hose or if a connection fails, just cut out the bad part and insert a new piece, using hose clamps on each side. Later you can replace the hose that failed.

This is as good a time as any to mention that *any* bolt (including the ones on the hose clamps) anywhere on the engine or related systems should be coated with an antiseizing compound (available from an autoparts store). This way you'll always be able to disassemble a system without needing to drill out and retap the holes.

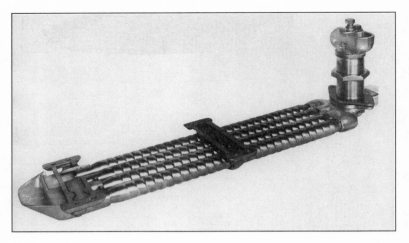

■ An external keel cooler can be used on wood, fiberglass, and, with proper bonding, metal hulls. This keel cooler is made by Walter Machine Company in New Jersey. They make models that will handle 10- to 5,000-horsepower engines. Photo courtesy of Walter Machine Co.

Saltwater-cooled manifolds in a freshwater-cooled system don't last as long as saltwater-cooled manifolds in a raw-water system, because the freshwater system runs at a higher temperature, which makes the salt crystallize. Some people say to replace manifolds in a system like this every three or four years, but this depends on the brand of manifold—and it's probably a good idea to ask your engine manufacturer about this, because if a manifold rusts through you'll be stopped dead. It may be possible to patch it back together with something like J.B. Weld or MarineTex, but this is a temporary repair at best.

To avoid these problems, you can use freshwater cooling for the exhaust manifolds by installing "risers" where the exhaust joins the rubber exhaust line. Raw water is directed to the riser where it cools the exhaust, but it remains separate from the actual manifold. These risers are relatively inexpensive and simple to replace. I've been taking the risers off the manifolds on my "product test boat," a Chris-Craft Sea Skiff, every 100 hours and inspecting them for deterioration. After 400 hours they seem as good as new.

This takes us to the issue of freshwater cooling versus raw-water cooling. After five years of dealing with a freshwater-cooled engine, I've come to some conclusions that aren't exactly mainstream.

Raw-water-cooled engines have a 140°F thermostat that keeps the seawater cool enough to prevent crystallization and salt deposits. Freshwater systems always use 160°F thermostats, because, goes the argument, the hotter the engine runs the more efficiently it runs (to a point) and the better the fuel economy.

Well, no one has yet explained to me exactly how much more efficiency or longevity you get from a hotter-running engine, and I've seen *lots* of really old raw-water-cooled engines, both gas and diesel, that were still running fine.

Since a raw-water cooling system is so much simpler and inexpensive to install than a freshwater system (with the exception of a sealed freshwater system with a dry exhaust) that cools the fresh water by pumping raw water through a heat exchanger, and since there are so many old raw-water-cooled engines out there demonstrating that low-temperature raw-water cooling doesn't kill an engine for years and years, I don't believe I'd install a freshwater cooling system at all.

I base this conclusion in part on observations from my product test boat, the old Chris Sea Skiff. This boat was a commercial salmon troller off the Oregon coast for about 20 years. The owner died, and the boat was left out on an eastern Oregon prairie to rot away. I came along and, being a sucker for stray dogs and old boats, bought it, trucked it home, and restored it.

It had the original raw-water-cooled engine and manifolds. The engine was seized, but this was because it had sat for five years or so out in the weather with the valve covers off. The manifolds themselves looked just fine.

I replaced the engine with a new V-8, and completely forgetting that I was replacing a raw-water-cooled engine that had run for 20 hard years and would still be running if it hadn't been stored in a snowdrift, I installed a freshwater cooling system. This system costs about $1,000, takes up 25 percent more space in the engine compartment, and requires more maintenance time than the engine itself.

A raw-water-cooled engine uses the engine's own internal steel water pump to suck in cooling water; it circulates the water inside the block, and it exits directly into the exhaust manifold. The freshwater system uses a separate, belt-driven pump with a rubber impeller and has hoses all over the place, leading to a heat exchanger and back to the exhaust riser—a lot of things to go wrong and wear out.

I've had more breakdowns due to the cooling system goofing up than I can remember. Perhaps some of these were my fault, because designing, installing, and living with the system has been a learning experience for me. And one thing I definitely learned is I don't want another cooling system like this.

When you uncrate your brand-new marine diesel you'll have all sorts of strong emotional and protective feelings and you'll want to do whatever you can to keep it happy and healthy. It's only natural to think freshwater cooling. I understand that; it's supposed to be the best, and most yachtsmen use it. But if I couldn't have a completely sealed freshwater system with a dry stack, I'd go with raw water. It's cheaper, simpler, more reliable, and from what I've seen it doesn't greatly diminish the life of an engine as long as you use a 140°F thermostat. Some people install a Y fitting where the raw-water line comes into the boat so they can attach a hose and flush out the engine with fresh water from time to time.

NOISE

BOATS SUFFER FROM TWO TYPES OF NOISE: mechanical (engine) noise and vibration-induced rattles. While both are annoying, I find rattling the worst. I *hate* rattles, whether in cars or in boats.

Engine noise is relatively easy to deal with. Use the best muffler system you can find, insulate the floor above the engine and the bulkheads on each side, and things will be fine. I was recently out on a 28-foot glass planing cruiser with a 200-horsepower turbocharged diesel mounted right under the house sole. When steering the boat you were standing a foot above and 2 feet to the side of the engine, but with the wet exhaust, big mufflers, and heavy-duty sound insulation, you could carry on a conversation in a normal tone of voice even with the engine running flat out. I hadn't believed such sound deadening was possible until I actually experienced it.

Then there's the matter of engine speed. As we saw in the graph a few pages back, as engine speed increases so too does fuel consumption, but with relatively small increases in boat speed. The same holds true of noise. The 6-71 Detroit Diesel's not so affectionate nickname, Screamin' Jimmy, must have been coined by someone running the engine at 1,800 RPM; throttle that same engine back to 1,200 RPMs, and it stops screaming and starts purring.

While it's practically impossible to eliminate all engine noise in powerboats, with insulation and attention to the exhaust system you can change a bothersome roar into a relaxing *hummmmm* rather easily, especially with the small diesels running at relaxed speeds typical of a Troller Yacht.

Rattles are a whole different problem. Rattling and vibration noises drive you crazy. These aren't the steady, soothing humming of a good engine doing its job but an irritating signal that something, somewhere, isn't right.

Fiberglass boats seem most susceptible to vibration noises. Fiberglass itself tends to broadcast sound, particularly such items as molded hatch lids and locker doors, which often are no more than 1/8 inch thick. This thin, flexible material may provide sufficient structural strength for the item in question, but if you think about it, it's also a damned good imitation of your stereo system's speaker cone: a thin, flexible material that amplifies sound waves. Rattles, in other words. Steel hulls can broadcast sound just as well, but steel doesn't flex as easily as fiberglass and so shows less tendency to amplify small vibrations into large rattles. Wood hulls are the quietest, as wood itself deadens sound, and two pieces of wood placed together won't rattle.

The best defense against vibration-induced rattles is to stop them before they start. If you have a glass or steel hull, the first step is to have it heavily insulated with foam. Steel boats usually have foam sprayed on during construction; glass hulls often have foam sheets glassed against the hull, and some glass hulls—foam-sandwich construction—have foam as an integral part of the layup. Personally, I'm not a great fan of most plastic boats, so I'm not up on the specifics of dealing with their idiosyncrasies.

Other vibration-induced rattles can be tracked down one by one and eliminated at the source. This might involve building heavier hatch covers, weather-stripping door or window seals, firmly tying down anything on deck, lining locker shelves with that plastic mesh stuff you see on the service areas of cocktail bars, and so on.

Some people even go to the extreme of using "soft" engine mounts and flexible shaft couplings, the idea being to absorb the engine's vibration rather than transmit it through the hull. I think soft mounting systems were developed to keep the engine from shaking the mounts out of lightly built glass hulls, but that's probably my anti-plastic prejudices coming through. I remember one boat that could have used them: a 36-foot heavy wood sailboat with a single-cylinder German diesel that thumped so hard, the vibration on deck made it nearly impossible to focus your eyes on objects ashore. Like the superquiet glass boat mentioned above, I didn't think this was possible, either.

You can familiarize yourself with the products for dealing with sound by visiting any good engine shop. You'll find everything from heavy rubberish paints and sticky-back sheets around 1/16 inch thick that can turn a bell ring into a dull clank all the way up to lead-backed insulation materials that flat-out absorb noise. Heavily insulate the engine-room bulkheads and sole, make all doors and deck fittings heavy enough not to rattle, and provide attachment systems that hold them securely in place. After that, tracking down and stopping annoying noises just becomes detective work.

Cruising boats have many other systems. If you carry a decent-size skiff you'll need a way to haul it out of the water. Then there are ventilation systems, navigation systems, sanitary systems, and probably other things that slip my mind. All of these can be handled in a variety of ways, but the best ways usually don't become evident until you've actually lived with your boat and stared at the problems for a while.

From Workboat
to Cruiser

IF YOU'RE INTERESTED ENOUGH in practical cruising powerboats like my Troller Yacht to have read this far, I'm guessing you've been interested in power cruisers for a while and probably have an idea what's available and what a typical production trawler yacht looks like. But in case you're coming from a straight sailing background and don't follow contemporary production powerboat stuff, but you've gotten interested in powerboats and you want to go down to the boat show and look at some boats along the lines I've been talking about in this book, let me save you a trip: At this writing there are no American production boats like these; most of what is being sold as cruising powerboats have more in common with deluxe motor homes than with seagoing boats.

This seems poised to change in the near future, because the concept of efficiently and economically cruising under power just makes too much sense, especially with all those aging baby-boomer sailors creaking around out there. A few designers are working on boats like these, and it's only a matter of time before a few of the small, high-end boatbuilders offer the first off-the-shelf power cruisers designed to cover long distances economically and comfortably.

But for now, if you want a boat to go seriously cruising under power (and I define this as ocean passagemaking), you'll either have to build a boat yourself or have one custom-built. And you'll face the additional problem of finding a design to build, since few contemporary designers seem interested in this field.

■ The 51-foot *Salute*, which began life as a U.S. Army torpedo chaser, was converted into a salmon and tuna troller in 1978. It has full electronics with two radars and a chart plotter, a Cat diesel, a refrigerated hold, and a comfortable living area with color TV. It was entirely refastened with stainless, and the boat is in top condition structurally and mechanically. In 1996 it was for sale, with all fishing licenses, for $75,000. The owner told me the only time he was uncomfortable aboard was in a 60-knot gale.

Of course, we can't forget that many small seagoing motorboats have been designed since the first engine was installed in a hull, and some have been wonderful. A few designers seemed to develop interesting craft consistently, perhaps because they were lucky in their commissions, although it's more likely much of the credit goes to their particular eye and philosophy.

One of my favorite designers has always been William Garden, and I blame my childhood discovery of him and his writing for hopelessly ruining me for a corporate career. Over his life, Garden has designed every conceivable type of boat, from 6-foot dinks to small ships. His designs can be found in many old boating magazines (back when all the magazines had design sections), numerous books of collected boat designs, and two books of his own (see Appendix IV). He is still turning out custom work from his office on an island in British Columbia.

Garden is of the old school of design, which means he's also a wonderful carpenter, and many of his designs are not simple to build, if costs are an issue. But many are, and in many cases those that aren't could be used as a basis for a new design, keeping the basic look but changing the reverse-curved S-sectioned hull to something simpler, or keeping the curves and building in ferrocement.

L. Francis Herreshoff is remembered as a sailboat designer, but he also designed some interesting powerboats. Herreshoff was a great advocate of simplicity, so it's surprising that most of his cruising power designs are twin screw; yet he didn't seem to trust even two engines, so they all have sail backup! If you build one, there's no reason you can't install only one engine. Many of his designs are featured in *Sensible Cruising Designs* (International Marine Publishing, 1973). One of my favorites is the Lifeboat Ketch, a 44- × 9-foot 6-inch double-ender that looks as though he took the basic U.S. Coast Guard surf rescue boat and made a yacht of it. This boat is really elegant and shows the proportional balance Herreshoff is known for; it's powered by twin 30-horsepower gas engines. Herreshoff always preferred gas to diesel because gas engines are quieter, smoother, and lighter weight. Of course for a voyaging boat, gasoline simply isn't practical. And today's diesels are far different from the diesels Herreshoff learned to hate!

Herreshoff's Marco Polo, the 55×10×5-foot 6-inch, 38,000-pound displacement three-masted motorsailer, has been built many times and cruised the world over. If you build one, leave off his free-hanging rudder and give the boat a rudder mounted on a skeg. Even the most brilliant designers go off on tangents, and this free-hanging rudder was a bad idea, easily damaged and making the boat squirrely to steer under power.

William Atkin is another designer remembered mainly for sail but who also turned out interesting power designs. Atkin was another of the old-time masters, and in his early days he ran a boatshop where he'd design and build the boat *and* the engine! He published hundreds of his designs over the years in the old *MotorBoating & Sailing,* many of which were later collected in book form (check libraries and used-book stores).

For a bit of historical trivia I'm rather proud of, I'm pretty sure I was the last person to sell a building plan to *MB&S.* In 1973, while in Monterey with the 26-foot sailboat I'd designed, I got talking to some tourist. I never got his name, but he knew Pete Smyth, then editor at *MB&S,* and he told me to send Pete the plans. Well, I did, along with a 50-page article that evolved into *Buehler's Backyard Boatbuilding* 20 years later. Smyth bought the plans and article for $400, a good month's salary in those days! They never did print the plans. I suspect Smyth bought them just to encourage me. He did that, all right. Rather than go into the army, where I'd either be a retired sergeant with a pension by now or assembling airplanes at Boeing, here I am still messing with boats.

There are many other designers, famous and unheard of, who have turned out interesting work. Look in the boating section of any big-city library and you'll find all sorts of design collections.

THE RIGHT HULL

O F COURSE THERE IS A LOGICAL OPTION to building a new boat: converting an existing boat. And that starts with finding the right hull.

I've seen a few power cruisers converted from sailboats, but find-

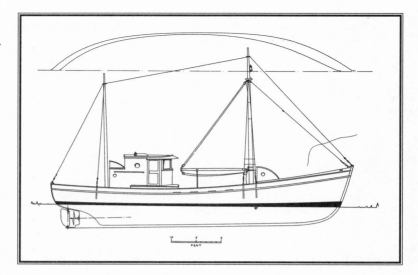

■ The New England sardine carrier is an excellent example of a fuel-efficient, seaworthy powerboat. Illustration from *Working Watercraft*, by Thomas Gilmer (1972).

ing a suitable hull isn't easy. For example, most will have a propeller aperture too small to handle an efficient prop; the engine will be too small or insufficiently rugged for running day after day; the fuel tanks will be too small; the deck structure will be all wrong, and there won't be a way to build-in a pilothouse; the house itself will be very low, which means the cabin sole will also be very low, with no room in the bilge. A sailboat's likely to have a deep hull with mostly outside ballast, but without the pressure from the sails this will give you a very quick and uncomfortable motion.

Of course there are some exceptions, one being to start off with a decent motorsailer. For example, William Hand designed some beauties, but I don't think I'd modify one of them; Hand's motorsailers are pretty close to being Troller Yachts, although with a bigger sailing rig than you'd need for continuous cruising under power.

To my mind, converting a sailboat to a powerboat will always be more expensive and more trouble than it's worth; you'd be money ahead starting from scratch. If you're still thinking conversion, a far better choice is a small commercial fishing boat.

As an industry, small-time commercial fishing is rapidly dying off in this country, regulated out of existence by forces that prefer the resource (what a government regulator calls a fish) be harvested (what a government regulator calls catching a fish) by a handful of very large, very high-tech, and very expensive boats instead of a large number of low-tech, family-owned boats. This may be a more efficient way to manage the "resource," but it's taken a terrible social toll, devastating coastal communities and destroying the tradition of family fishing.

We're always hearing about the plight of the family farm, but the family fishing business has been hit far harder, with nary a peep from

■ The 72-foot *Aquavit* was saved by laminating a plywood skin to her shot bottom planking. I wouldn't head around Cape Stiff in her, but she's fine for summer coasting and Northwest cruising. Photo by Stacia Green.

Willie Nelson or Jesse Jackson. And the related businesses that supported the fishing industry have been killed off, too: the chandleries, the canneries, the marine railways, the engine mechanics, and all the other little businesses that kept the local fleet working. Our coastal communities are dying with them, too, surviving today as little more than tourist destinations.

But, well . . . all this means there are some damned good buys on small workboats out there, and some of them could be converted into damned good cruisers at relatively low cost. Everything's there. The engine might need overhauling, at least before you head across an ocean, but you *have* an engine, all installed. You also have the running gear and steering gear, anchoring systems and ground tackle, a galley, likely a head, lighting, heating, navigation, pumps, and so on. The whole boat. You'll almost certainly have to gut the interior and redo it, and in smaller boats you'll want to tear out the hold and build in a cabin. With a bigger boat, say 50 feet or so, you can use the hold as a shop or for storage.

Most areas of the country evolved some form of seaworthy and fuel-efficient workboat. Many fine boats in the 35- to 60-foot range were built of the very best materials for the military, and many are in use today as cruisers. A lot of Gulf Coast shrimpers are around, but for the most part these are real tubs, fat and shallow, but their predecessors, the sailing sloops and schooners, would make fine power cruisers. I doubt many originals are left, but my friend Mike Boussard, in

Pass Christian, Mississippi, builds new ones, and his latest one is fitted out as a power cruiser.

In New England, the old swordfishing boats have potential, and one of the finest seagoing boats ever built, not to mention one of the most beautiful, is the New England sardine carrier. Like the West Coast salmon trollers, these boats weren't designed to carry huge amounts of fish over short distances and so weren't as burdensome as the New England draggers. Because they had to cruise often long distances carrying herring from the weirs back to the canneries, they needed to be fuel efficient. And they had to be very seaworthy, because they worked off the temperamental New England coast from spring through December. Most ran somewhere between 55 and 60 feet long, with a 15-foot beam and a 5-foot draft. They move so easily, even loaded, that 150 horsepower was considered sufficient, even when carrying tons of fish. Back in the early 1970s, a Seattle fisherman and his wife brought one out to Seattle via the Panama Canal, and they had only good things to say about their new boat.

■ The mid-30-footer *Edison* is pretty, but boy is she roly-poly. The asking price was $17,000, but she had a gas engine, no anchor winch, and no electronics. I'd offer $10,000 tops.

Of course my favorites are the West Coast trollers, and while a few guys still earn a living trolling, the fishery is essentially dead except in Alaska, and the resale value of a troller is very low. I keep half an eye out and recently looked at one, the *Edison,* with an asking price of $17,000. Another, the *Terry M.,* a real heavy-duty 42-footer in fine condition that even had full electronics, was $25,000. Both could almost certainly be bought for three-quarters of the asking price, and maybe less.

If you see a troller that strikes your fancy, before anything else give it the "roll test." Some of these boats were built with real barrel midsections and roll like drunken sailors unless they're fully loaded and have their trolling poles and flopper-stoppers extended. You can get a hint of this just walking the decks, but to really check it out, stand on the dock next to the boat, hold on to a stay bracing the mast or trolling pole, and pull. While any boat will lean some, a roly-poly hull will easily lean toward you. When I saw *Edison* at the dock, I really started thinking about making an offer, but the roll test saved me; the poor boat rolled worse than anything I've ever seen. A few tons of concrete in the bilge would have slowed that down, of course, but I'd rather start off with something a bit more stable. Besides, as handsome as she was, *Edison* had a bit too much freeboard and lacked the grace of a boat like *Frances,* shown on page 24. If I ever convert a troller it's going to be the *perfect* troller, and there are some beauties out there!

SURVEYING

THESE BOATS ARE ALL OLD, but many are still structurally sound because they were built from top-quality materials. But you need to be tough and skeptical when looking, and unless you're very experienced with wood boats you'll need to hire a surveyor and have the boat hauled out for the inspection.

This is harder than it sounds. Marine surveyors run the spectrum from the blind to the clairvoyant. You need no license or credentials to say you're a surveyor, nor do you need to pass an exam. There is an organization of surveyors that accredit themselves, but since anybody can say he's a surveyor, joining the surveyor's guild doesn't mean you know anything.

The people in the local boat-repair yard will know which surveyors are worth hiring, because they see their work. Even so, there's an old-boy network in the yards, too, so after getting a name at the shipyard it doesn't hurt to talk to the local bank and insurance company to see who they use. Banks and insurance companies that work with commercial boats have lists of competent surveyors they've worked with.

Surveying a wood boat is highly technical, and it's very easy to make mistakes because there are so many places on a boat that can't be seen—behind the tanks, for instance. But a good surveyor will get a feel for what's happening by looking in other areas, and by noticing any mold in the area or a differently colored bolt head or maybe some dampness underneath something, and he will write down any suspicions or gut feelings he has. A good report will mention the areas he couldn't inspect, with comments. For instance, you might read, *"The inner hull behind the tanks was inaccessible for inspection; however, close inspection of the areas immediately next to the tanks showed no signs of deterioration. The outside appearance of the hull planking in the tank area is smooth and tight, implying no broken frames or loose fastenings in that area."* If you read statements like that you know the guy thought about it, knows what he's doing, and is probably correct.

On many wood boats, the entire inside of the hull is sheathed with a light layer of planking. When I was surveying I hated to see that because I had no way of inspecting the frames. But again, careful examination of the outside of the hull will provide some clues. You might read, *"The inner hull sheathing made inspection of the frames impossible. Examination of the outer planking showed hard plank edges at the turn of the bilge, 19 to 24 feet aft of the bow, implying either deteriorated fastenings or broken frames in that area. The sheathing in this area should be removed to allow a more detailed examination."* If you read that, then you'd better make a detailed examination, or at least let your bid reflect the possible work.

In the 1970s, food-handling laws required that fish holds be lined and isolated from the rest of the boat. Until then the fish were dumped against the hull planking or sheathing in an area set off by bulkheads. After a trip, the hold would be washed out with pumped-in seawater, and some old-timers used to spray down the planks with diesel fuel. The salt water and diesel absolutely pickled the wood, so the odds are the hull behind the fish hold is good. Just as in the tank area, however, examining the outside of the hull provides a clue, but you won't know for sure what kind of shape things are in until you rip out the hold lining.

A few hull fastenings should be pulled and examined. Most of these boats were galvanized-fastened and probably will need refastening. This isn't such a big job, but it needs to be figured in before you decide to buy the boat. The big bolts in the backbone are probably all right. They can be very hard to pull for an examination, however, so if I were redoing a fishboat, I'd install a few new keel bolts when I had the interior gutted out, just on general principals.

All surveyors worry about litigation if they're wrong about something (that's why I quit), and some write elaborate disclaimers after their report, thinking this will protect them. It doesn't, by the way. But what it does do is give you a feel for the surveyor's confidence in his abilities.

I always ended my report the way I would want it to read if I had hired me. I was supposed to know what I was doing, so my disclaimer read: "Submitted without prejudice, this report is accurate to the best of my knowledge." However, many surveyors use a disclaimer they got from the how-to-be-a-marine-surveyor books that say, and I'm not making this up: "Not responsible for omission, misrepresentation, or misstatement of facts." If you translate that disclaimer into plain English, it says: "I'm not responsible for leaving out things, glossing over things because I'm actually being paid off by the seller, or outright lying." In my opinion, any surveyor who ends his survey with a disclaimer like that can't be trusted. He's saying so himself!

Most surveys just cover the boat's basic structure. Mechanical inspections other than the obvious (Is the steering working? The engine off its mounts?) require a person up on that particular stuff. You can listen to the engine run and do a compression test, but you really need to draw some oil and transmission fluid and have it analyzed by a testing lab (check the Yellow Pages). Wiring isn't that big of a concern, because you'll be redoing it all anyway. A wheelhouse full of exotic electronic stuff designed for fish-finding probably will get scrapped or sold, too.

Remember, you're responsible for any damage done to the boat during the inspection, and if you don't buy the boat you must fix what you've done. Basic courtesy and honesty (and intelligence; some of these old fishermen are damned tough guys and don't use lawyers to settle disputes) should make this obvious, but don't expect the seller to allow a survey until he's received a decent "earnest money" deposit, which can be used to put the boat back in the same shape as before the survey if the deal goes sour. I watched one surveyor cut a hole in the bottom of a boat; the buyer changed his mind, and the poor owner was stuck.

Surveying out a 40-foot boat should take at least several hours, and a good job could take half a day. Don't buy a boat until you see the written report; you might have questions.

After saying all this, I doubt I'd ever really convert a workboat myself, because I learned years back that it's easier to build a simple new boat than try to rework an old one; if you compare the actual costs involved, starting from scratch is usually much cheaper. And you end up with a new boat rather than a reworked old boat.

Still, I could see doing it if you ran across just the right boat, priced right and in really good shape. You could play around with it for a few years, make a trip or two, and see if you really liked power cruising. It's one thing to read books; it's quite another to get out there and do it Your own experience would give you a better idea of what you really want in a serious cruising boat. Besides, you would have saved some nice old boat from the wreckers, guaranteeing entrance to Paradise!

NEW LIVES FOR OLD HULLS: A CASE STUDY

THERE ARE A LOT OF OLD WORKBOATS out there, and many are going for extremely low prices. But remember, no more than a handful of wood trollers or swordfishermen or sardine carriers have been built since the 1960s. And even fewer have been built since the 1940s to the old-time designs on which I've based my Troller Yachts. Some of these boats are still in great shape, but most are getting pretty tired.

But there is a simple and inexpensive system that will add years of life to a tired boat: covering the entire hull with a new skin. This is worth doing even with a healthy wood boat, as it will ensure it remains leak-free and will lower its maintenance requirements.

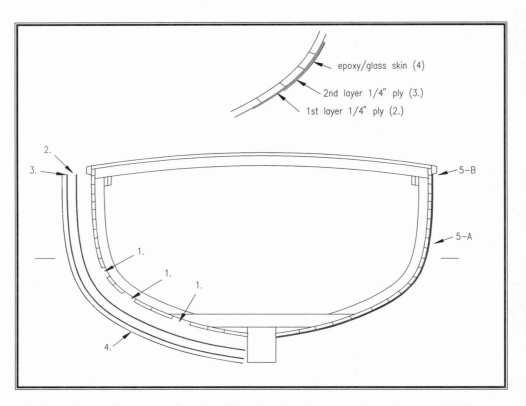

epoxy/glass skin (4)

2nd layer 1/4" ply (3.)

1st layer 1/4" ply (2.)

2.

3.

5–B

5–A

1.

1.

1.

4.

■ A plywood skin will extend the life of an old wooden boat. It can also be used on a sound hull to reduce maintenance because the plywood with epoxy skin isolates the original hull.
1) Replace any bad planks. Since the area will be covered, use only a good-quality construction lumber; no need for "boat grade." 2) The first layer of ¼-inch plywood is glued with a sticky mastic (like asphalt roof patch) and nailed to the hull. You can stop about 4 inches above the waterline (5-A) or continue to the sheer (5-B). I would stop just above the waterline in most cases. Continue to the sheer only if the topsides are in bad condition. If continuing to the sheer, stop at the rubrail. 3) A second layer of plywood is glued and nailed to the first layer. 4) Glass cloth is then stapled to the hull and soaked down with epoxy. This step can be skipped since there are new industrial coatings that will protect the plywood. The boat on which we used this fix has been in the water three years now without epoxy, and so far there's no sign of deterioration in the plywood. However, the epoxy can't hurt anything, especially below the waterline.

Following is an account of our experiences applying a new skin to an old boat.

The 72-foot *Aquavit* was built in Canada for American gangsters who used it to smuggle booze during Prohibition. After getting busted by the Coast Guard, she became a yacht. Her three 12-cylinder gas engines were replaced with a single GMC 6-71 diesel, and for the last 60 years she's been everything from a family cruiser to a logging-camp bunkhouse. Three years ago my friend Fred read about her being for sale. The eagerness of her owner to make a deal should have warned him, but Fred was driven mad by boat-lust.

A surveyor, either blind or crooked or both, pronounced the old boat sound, and on his word Fred bought it. Then, as Fred headed off for lunch, the shipyard that hauled the boat for the survey suggested they remove a plank and inspect the frames. Whether the result was a total misunderstanding or whether the shipyard is owned by crooks we'll never know, but when Fred came back from lunch several planks were off (and sawed into 6-inch lengths so they couldn't be reused!), and Fred was told it would cost about $60,000 to put her back together again. Even then, the yard said it wouldn't guarantee the job because the boat was so old.

Fred was about ready to just abandon the boat, but decided to come talk to me about it first. I suggested that, if he was so hot to save this boat, he try a low-tech "fix": laminating on a new skin that would stop the leaks, and stiffen and strengthen the structure.

I'd first seen this done in 1970 down in San Francisco, where a ferrocement skin was added to an old tug being converted into a sailing ship. Nowadays this is done by "cold-molding" two or three layers of thin cedar planks set in epoxy on top of an existing hull, and it's becoming almost commonplace. This isn't exactly inexpensive, though, and it takes a lot of work, so this fix is normally only done if the existing hull is basically sound but a little tired. Maybe old age has loosened up everything and it's working a little and so always leaks a bit. Maybe the boat was lightly built and the owner wants to use it for long-range cruising, and figures adding ½ inch of thickness to the skin will make it safer. Or maybe the owner is tired of the annual ritual of sanding and painting and caulking and wants an epoxy skin that is unaffected by marine growth, swelling, and shrinking, and can be painted with one of the new superhard, long-lasting paints such as linear polyurethane. People are cold-molding new skins on boats for all sorts of reasons, and it has withstood the test of time. Tim and Pauline Carr, for example, cold-molded a new skin over their century-old Falmouth Quay punt *Curlew,* and have since circumnavigated a time or two and spent five or six years cruising the Antarctic, the Falkland Islands, and the Island of South Georgia in all seasons with no trouble at all. But *Curlew* was in pretty good shape to begin with.

Fred's situation was a bit different. His boat had big holes in it, half the frames were rotted, and it was essentially dead. He had to do something quick to get out of that yard before they took all his money, plus we didn't want to add any more weight than we needed to. That ruled out concrete; it's slow to work and heavy. It also seemed to rule out traditional cold-molding, because it too is slow and expensive, and usually must be done under cover.

The round-bilge hull didn't have any extreme reverse curves, so I thought that maybe adding two layers of ¼-inch plywood was the way to go. It's amazing how much you can wrap 1/4-inch ply if you don't know you're not supposed to be able to do it; if you do get stuck, you can cut pieces into triangular shapes that can be fitted just about anywhere. With the butts of the two layers overlapped and the old planking to fasten into, you can easily lay on the plywood without worrying about individual sizes or placements.

Unfortunately, the yard got in on this job, too, and convinced Fred to put a layer of tar paper between the first layer of ply and the hull. This kind of sheathing is nothing new. In the old sailing-ship days, sheathing was used to protect ships from teredo worms. To protect the original hull, the early shipbuilders applied a layer of tar paper, or "Irish linen" as it's called in the shipyards, adding a sacrificial layer of thin planking over that. But we weren't looking to apply worm sheathing; we needed to strengthen a shot hull with two layers of plywood, and to achieve the greatest strength both layers need to be attached to the original hull.

The proper way to do this job is to remove the hull's paint with a disc sander, spread a thick layer of mastic on the bare hull, and nail or screw down the plywood over that. An adhesive mastic does a great job of locking the plywood securely to the hull. The cheapest and probably the stickiest mastic is simple roofing cement. This sticky black stuff, known as "bear shit" in the shipyards, costs about seven bucks a gallon and will stick to anything.

Unfortunately, the tar-paper layer the shipyard insisted on applying prevented the mastic from sticking Fred's plywood directly to his planking, and this has caused some problems, which I'll get to soon.

Here's how the job was done. First, the missing planks were replaced. We used plain 2 × 6 Douglas-fir house lumber, because with a new skin going over the planking we didn't need boat-grade stuff and the fit didn't have to be perfect. Then the yard tacked on that damned layer of tar paper (don't do this). Then enough goop was spread to cover the area equal to a sheet of ply; the plywood was held against the hull and nailed or screwed down. The second layer of ply was installed over the first, staggering the joints and using the same goop to bond the second layer to the first. The plywood was carried up about 6 inches above the waterline, and the raw edge was covered by a 4-inch-wide strip of ironbark. The hull was primed and painted, then launched. No epoxy or fiberglass was used over the plywood.

We used fir marine plywood because Fred got a good buy, but we could have just as easily used normal exterior grade, possibly covered with a layer of epoxy/glass sheathing. There are alternatives to epoxy/glass, such as various industrial coatings, that are cheaper and easier to apply if you don't need the additional strength of epoxy/glass.

I seem to hear almost daily about some new kind of paint or

chemical that does something wonderful like deaden noise, make something nonslip, destroy rust, or whatever. You can learn about new products in the marine world by reading commercial boat magazines like *Workboat, Pacific Fisherman,* or *Marine Reporter,* to name a few. *Boats & Harbors,* published in Crossville, Tennessee, is a newsprint collection of marine-related classified ads that comes out three time a month and is well worth subscribing to if you're building or restoring a boat.

Aquavit has been in the water for three years since this "fix" and seems to be doing all right. A small section of plywood just above the prop did tear off, but we suspect this was because the yard's tar-paper layer prevented the mastic from bonding the ply to the hull. We patched the area with new ply and mastic (and no tar paper), and next time he hauls, Fred is going to cover the area subject to prop wash with epoxy/glass.

A boat like *Aquavit* in mint condition would cost half a million dollars or more, making it out of the question for most of us. Fred paid $32,000 for the boat (*way* too much, as he immediately learned), and the fix described here cost only a few thousand bucks for materials.

Of course, if you're planning on voyaging around Cape Horn you want your boat as strong as possible, so if the hull you buy is as tired as *Aquavit's* you might want to apply four layers of ply in mastic, extending them up to the sheer and adding another two layers to the deck for good measure. You'd have virtually the strength of a new boat.

So if you see a great buy on some grand but tired old ship, remember Fred! A few sheets of plywood and a little roofing tar will quickly and inexpensively add years of life to the old girl.

Understanding Plans and Estimating Costs

THERE'S SO MUCH HAPPENING in the world of custom boat design, it's amazing that so little of it receives national attention (although I suspect this might have something to do with custom builders and designers not buying full-page four-color ads in national magazines). People today have come to think that buying a boat has to be the same as buying a car: You just go down to the showroom and pick one out. Well, that is one option, but there are still hundreds of custom boatbuilding shops around the country, any one of which can often build you a better boat than a stock production boat for the same price or less. This way you can choose whatever design you want and also oversee the construction and arrange everything about the boat exactly as you'd like.

If you want a Troller Yacht, you almost have to build a new boat, since few used ones are available, and at this writing there are no production-built examples. Even finding the building plans for one is going to take some searching. Over the years, many fine cruising powerboats and motorsailers have been built, and spending time in a good library or boating bookstore will give you all sorts of leads. Some of the design anthologies are good places to look, as are tribute books to recently departed designers. Maybe you'll get lucky and find a printed plan of a boat that's perfect for you. At the least you'll get ideas you can use when you hire a designer to draw your plans.

It's important to become knowledgeable before you go looking for a designer. Right off the bat, if you know what you want you'll learn

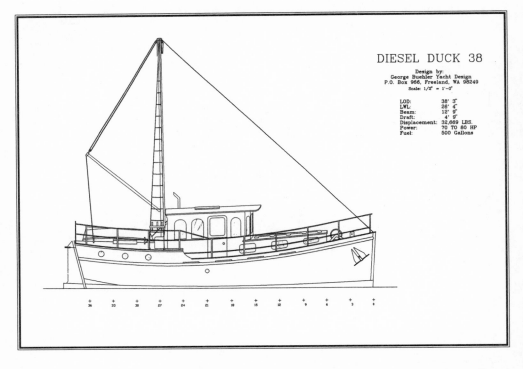

DIESEL DUCK 38

Design by:
George Buehler Yacht Design
P.O. Box 966, Freeland, WA 98249

Scale: 1/2" = 1'-0"

LOD: 38' 3"
LWL: 28' 4"
Beam: 12' 9"
Draft: 4' 9"
Displacement: 32,669 LBS.
Power: 70 TO 80 HP
Fuel: 500 Gallons

■ Diesel Duck 38
plan: profile

whether or not you can work with the guy. If he criticizes the stuff you give him, it doesn't necessarily mean that *you* are wrong. And it will save time in the design process, because you're showing him right off what you want and you'll avoid wasting time and money with inappropriate preliminary proposals.

Where do you find a designer? All over! But first, it might be useful to know the difference between a "yacht designer" and a "naval architect."

A Naval Architect has a four-year or better engineering degree in Naval Architecture and Marine Engineering. Only a few colleges offer this highly technical degree, and the courses are oriented much more toward designing warships and ocean liners than small cruising boats. In most cases, anything a degree-holding Naval Architect might know about small boats he picked up on his own. Some self-taught and correspondence-school guys add the initials "N.A." after their names, but it must mean something other than Naval Architect, because without the degree you ain't one.

A Yacht Designer is a person who designs boats. To call yourself a Yacht Designer, you don't need a marine engineering degree, you don't need a license, and you don't need to meet certain standards.

The same holds true of the shoreside equivalent. An Architect is a degree-holding engineer who designs buildings. A designer is someone without a degree who designs buildings. Most pleasure boats are

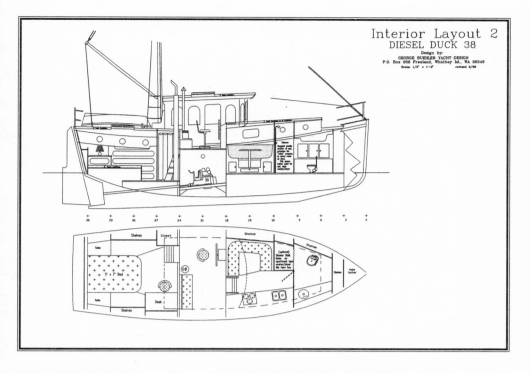

Interior Layout 2
DIESEL DUCK 38

Design by:
GEORGE BUEHLER YACHT ·DESIGN
P.O. Box 966 Freeland, Whidbey Isl., WA 98249
Scale: 1/2" = 1'-0"   revised 8/96

designed by Yacht Designers, not degree-holding Naval Architects (A bit of historical trivia: Weston Farmer, who I believe helped create the first Naval Architecture courses offered in this country, called them "nasal artichokes."), and this holds true for most of the great names in yacht design: Hand, Herreshoff, Alden, Atkin, and so on.

In my case, I had absolutely no interest in designing an aircraft carrier, so even if I had been academically inclined I wouldn't have gone after a N.A. degree. For me, hanging around boatyards and working as a floor sweeper and wood butcher formed a perfect education, because I learned firsthand how boats are built. Cruising in boats and generally playing with them showed me what they needed to look like and how various designs performed. This is of course very unscientific, but this is the traditional way Yacht Designers learned the trade, first working in the yards to learn how to build boats, then learning drafting and beginning to design. Many of the great builders were also great designers. For example, Nathanael Herreshoff is remembered both for the outstanding quality of the boats his company built and for his outstanding designs.

I'm lucky enough to have been young at a time when lots of custom builders were still around, so I was able to get a bit of "traditional eddication." Today this is pretty hard to do. A few correspondence courses do teach boat design, but many people taking those classes have no building experience, and their design work often reflects that.

■ **Diesel Duck 38 plan: interior**

continued on page 132

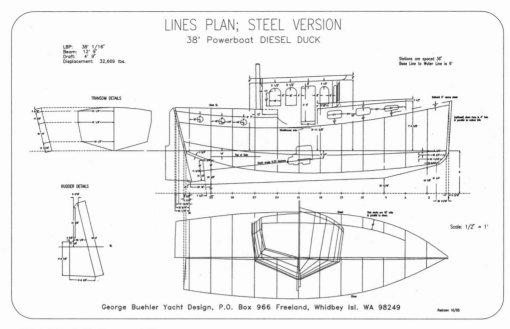

■ Diesel Duck 38 plan: steel lines

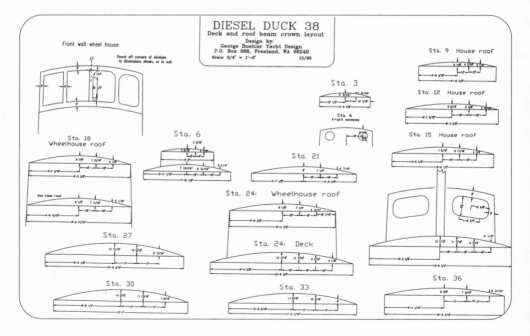

■ Diesel Duck 38 plan: deck beam layouts

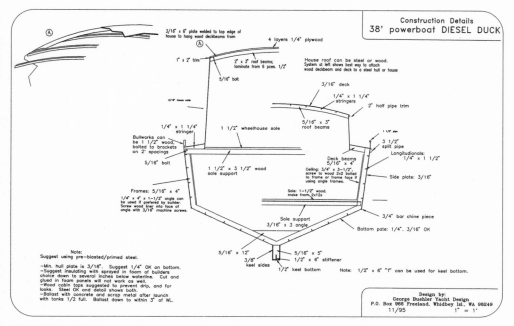

■ Diesel Duck 38 plan: steel construction cross section

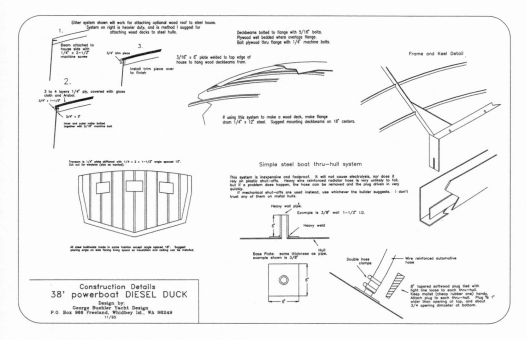

■ Diesel Duck 38 plan: steel construction details

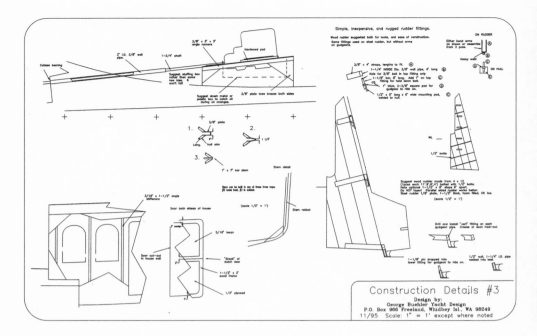

Construction Details #3
Design by:
George Buehler Yacht Design
P.O. Box 966 Freeland, Whidbey Isl., WA 98249
11/95 Scale: 1" = 1' except where noted

■ Diesel Duck 38 plan: steel construction details

You can find boat designs in the classified ads of boating magazines. Most designers (I'm including N.A.s in this term, now) offer catalogs or portfolios that detail their services and show previous designs.

The fun (and the money) in design work is with custom design, but most designers offer stock plans for greatly reduced fees. Stock plans are completed building plans that usually began life as a custom design; they're relatively inexpensive because all the designer has to do is run off blueprints and mail them out.

Sometimes you'll see a stock design that is almost what you want. In this case most designers will be happy to work with you to make whatever changes you want. Of course you'll pay for his time, but you'll pay less than for a custom design.

Plans fees are all over the map, with most designers charging what the market will bear. Here's how pricing works: A designer starts low and raises prices until the plans stop selling; then he lowers them a bit. A really busy designer in great demand can charge more than a designer who is unknown or isn't currently in fashion.

Prices for stock plans run from several hundred dollars up to $5,000 or more, and "designer" designers like Sparkman & Stephens or the like can add an extra zero or more to the price. Custom designing seems to start somewhere under $1,000 and runs steeply up from there. The most expensive custom design I've heard of was $300,000 for a 70-footer. But for this fee, the designers drew out absolutely everything: every wire, every pipe connection; I understand they even designed the steering wheel. Now that's the kind of commission most

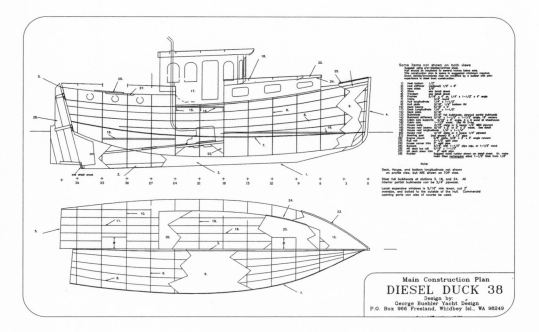

Main Construction Plan
DIESEL DUCK 38
Design by:
George Buehler Yacht Design
P.O. Box 966 Freeland, Whidbey Isl., WA 98249

■ **Diesel Duck 38 plan: steel construction plan**

of us dream about. You'd draw the basic boat, then just hire some young engineer to figure out the details; over the next six months you could call in on the cruise ship's satellite phone to see how he's coming along.

If you have some familiarity with boats and the confidence to work on your own, there's no reason you can't design your own or at least modify an existing plan. For instance, there's no need to pay somebody to change an interior. Just draw in what you want. Lengthening or shortening a design is easy; just change the station spacing. Of course doing this will effect such things as the engine shaft angle, the rigging dimensions, and possibly the tank layout. These problems can be solved, however, and there's nothing mystical about it.

Several excellent books about boat design are available. One of my favorites is *Yacht Designing and Planning*, by Howard Chapelle (W. W. Norton, 1995). Armed with this book, a scale rule, some basic instruments, and a little confidence, you can make whatever modifications you want. And if the boat works out okay, you can go into the boat design business. That's how many of us started.

The definition of a "complete" set of plans depends on the designer. Obviously, a basic set of plans needs to contain enough information to build the boat. The degree of detail might depend on whether the building is being done by an amateur or by a seasoned pro, as I've found some professional yards want everything specced out completely while a home builder will just do things the way he wants. Speccing out everything can jack up the plans price, but an amateur

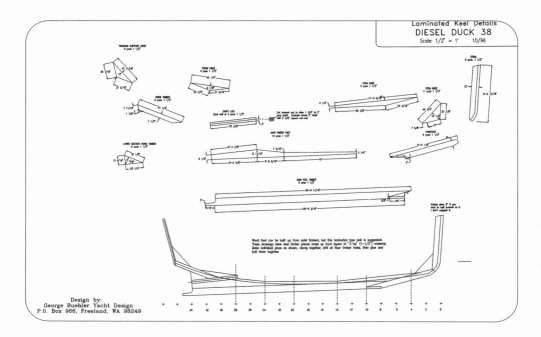

Design by:
George Buehler Yacht Design
P.O. Box 966, Freeland, WA 98249

■ Diesel Duck 38 plan: wood keel details

can figure out where each wire and through-hull and pipe goes with a little head scratching, and a pro is likely to do things exactly as he always has, no matter what the plans say. And frankly, if the designer doesn't have a solid construction background, you'll usually be better off figuring out where to put these kinds of things yourself.

Lofting a boat—drawing it out full size—is the easiest part of building, but for some reason it scares a lot of people. Some designers advertise "full-size patterns!" as though this were something special and a way out of lofting. It isn't. The only full-size patterns I've seen that would really make a difference in ease of construction are those meant for CAM (Computer-Aided Manufacturing). In this case, every piece of the boat is drawn on screen by some poor CAD operator, and full-size patterns are output onto Mylar or something similar. This costs as much as $10,000 for a boat in the mid-40s range, and according to an experienced professional builder I know, it isn't cost effective unless you're planning a production run of three or more boats.

What you usually see advertised as full-size patterns are just patterns for the frames. But there's much more to building a boat than just cutting out the frames, and almost all those pieces will require patterns, or at least they'll have to be laid out full size. You'll need to loft the stem profile, the keel, the transom, the house sides, the rudder. And of course with a metal hull you'll want plate patterns. It's unlikely that "full-size patterns" includes all this stuff. Unless you're willing to pay for CAD/CAM full-size patterns for every piece in the

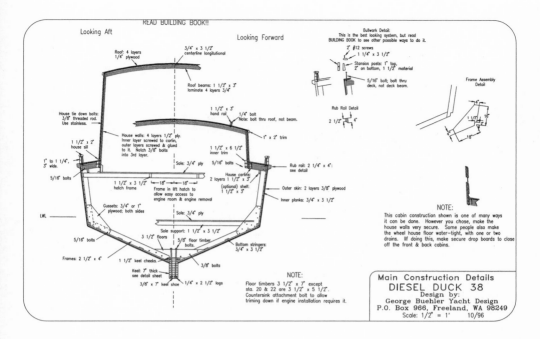

Looking Aft

Looking Forward

Bulwork Detail:
This is the best looking system, but read
BUILDING BOOK to see other possible ways to do it.

Roof: 4 layers
1/4" plywood

3/4" x 3 1/2"
centerline longitudinal

2" #12 screws
1 1/4" x 3 1/2"

Stansion posts: 1" top,
2" on bottom, 1 1/2" material

Frame Assembly
Detail

Roof beams: 1 1/2" x 3"
laminate 4 layers 3/4"

5/16" bolt; bolt thru
deck, not deck beam.

House tie down bolts:
3/8" threaded rod.
Use stainless.

1 1/2" x 3"
hand rail   1/4" bolt
Note: bolt thru roof, not beam.

Rub Rail Detail

2 1/2"   4"

House walls: 4 layers 1/2" ply.
Inner layer screwed to carlin,
outer layers screwed & glued
to it. Notch 3/8" bolts
into 3rd layer.

1 1/2" x 2"
house sil

1" x 2" trim

1 1/2" x 6 1/2"
inner trim

1" to 1 1/4",
3" wide.

5/16" bolts

Sole: 3/4" ply   5/16" bolts

House carlins:
2 layers 1 1/2" x 3"

Rub rail: 2 1/4" x 4":
see detail

1 1/2" x 3 1/2"
hatch frame

18"   18"

Frame in lift hatch to
allow easy access to
engine room & engine removal

(optional) shelf:
1 1/2" x 3"

Outer skin: 2 layers 3/8" plywood

Inner planks: 3/4" x 3 1/2"

Gussets: 3/4" or 1"
plywood; both sides

Sole: 3/4" ply

LWL

5/16" bolts

Sole support: 1 1/2" x 3 1/2"

3 1/2" floors   5/8" floor timber
bolts.

Bottom stringers:
3/4" x 3 1/2"

Frames: 2 1/2" x 4"

1 1/2" keel cheeks.

3/8" bolts

Keel: 7" thick
see detail sheet

3/8" x 7" keel shoe   1/4" x 2 1/2" logs

NOTE:
This cabin construction shown is one of many ways
it can be done. However you chose, make the
house walls very secure. Some people also make
the wheel house floor water-tight, with one or two
drains. IIf doing this, make secure drop boards to close
off the front & back cabins.

NOTE:
Floor timbers 3 1/2" x 7" except
sta. 20 & 22 are 3 1/2" x 5 1/2".
Countersink attachment bolt to allow
triming down if engine installation requires it.

Main Construction Details
DIESEL DUCK 38
Design by:
George Buehler Yacht Design
P.O. Box 966, Freeland, WA 98249
Scale: 1/2" = 1'   10/96

boat, you're simply going to have to loft it.

There's nothing to it! All the dimensions are provided in the plans. All you need to do is measure the distances from the offsets, make a mark, then connect all the marks with a line. You'll find one of the most thorough descriptions of lofting ever done in Howard Chapelle's great book, *Boatbuilding* (W. W. Norton, 1941, 1994); this is quite literally the bible of wood boatbuilding. In my opinion, you'll find the most easily understood description of lofting in, if you'll forgive me, *Buehler's Backyard Boatbuilding* (International Marine, 1991). After you learn lofting basics by reading my book, go back and read Chapelle's.

■ **Diesel Duck 38 plan: wood construction cross section**

READING PLANS

TO ILLUSTRATE WHAT TO EXPECT and look for in a set of plans, I've included the complete building plans for a Diesel Duck 38 in this chapter. (both composite wood and steel versions). I don't normally spec out the wiring or piping or other miscellaneous details, because exactly what you use and where you put it doesn't really matter, as long as it's adequate. Generally, I don't care what brand of what you put where. Other designers use words like "appropriate" or "to be done to standards as laid out by the ABYC (American Boat and Yacht Council)." A good one I saw recently was, "to be built, installed, and rated to suit the purpose intended."

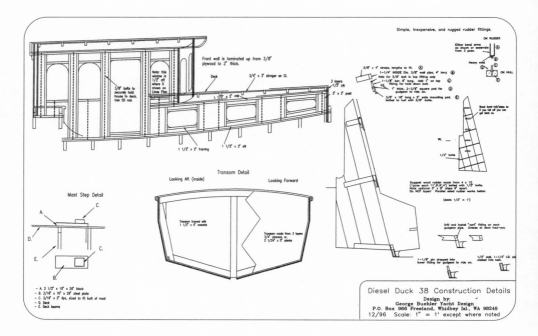

Diesel Duck 38 Construction Details
Design by:
George Buehler Yacht Design
P.O. Box 966 Freeland, Whidbey Isl., WA 98249
12/96 Scale: 1" = 1' except where noted

■ Diesel Duck 38 plan: wood construction details

Whatever the detail level, most plans will include the following:

1. *Lines Plan and Table of Offsets.* The *hull lines* are all the dimensions of the basic boat. Along with the *table of offsets,* the *lines plan* provides all the dimensions needed to build the boat: the frame or station dimensions, the house and windows, the engine shaft angle—everything. Sometimes more dimensioning is needed. This boat, for example, has a specific deck camber, so all the deck beams are laid out for the builder. Normally only a single beam would be shown on the main lines plan, and all beams will be made to that camber.

2. *Construction Detail Plan(s).* At least one sheet should show a basic construction cross section. The more details the better, of course, although many details are actually generic and not designed for a specific boat. For example, parts of the plan might be labeled something like, "typical through-hull (or exhaust or whatever) setup." But it should have specifics regarding the actual construction of the boat.

3. *Construction Plan.* This sheet will show a view of the boat minus its hull skin, giving you an idea how all the pieces go together.

4. *Specific Systems Plan(s).* These cover such stuff as the tanks, sail plan, and anything else "big."

5. *Interior Plan.* This shows the boat's living spaces. Some designers

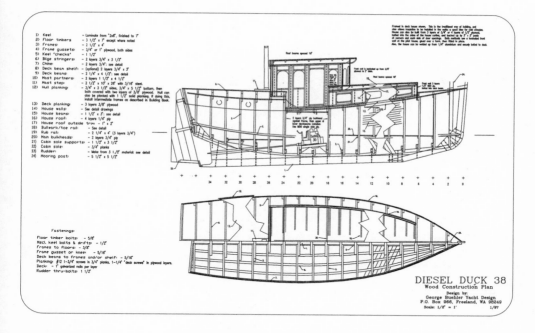

dimension everything, but I usually don't; in my experience, everybody changes things as they build.

■ **Diesel Duck 38 plan: wood construction plan**

Obviously I'm not impartial, but I think this is a good set of plans, illustrating all the important stuff. By the way, these plans were drafted with AutoCad, the industry-standard Computer-Aided Design program.

Costs

BUILDING COSTS DEPEND on how much of the building you're willing to do yourself, how resourceful you are at hunting out deals, and how you outfit the boat. A solid, seamanlike, fully outfitted 45-footer can easily be built for under $40,000 1998 dollars, if you do everything yourself. A client of mine recently finished a 67-foot wood schooner powered by a 4-71 Jimmy and spent only $35,000. He built it all himself and made no compromises in strength, basic systems, or looks—especially looks. In fact, this schooner's working-boat aura makes it just about the most awesome thing I've seen in quite a while. This may be a no-frills boat—there's not even pressure water on board—but it is one hell of a seagoing boat, the kind of boat where a man can walk the decks and feel, well, Manly, for want of a better word, and it doesn't matter which of the several genders you identify with.

I know talk like this tends to alienate folks with lots of money. After all, numerous mid-40s production boats are going for around

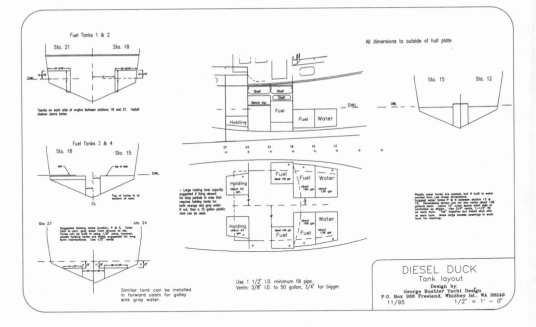

Fuel Tanks 1 & 2

Sta. 21   Sta. 18

All dimensions to outside of hull plate

Tanks on each side of engine between stations 18 and 21. Install
shelves above tanks.

Fuel Tanks 3 & 4

Sta. 18   Sta. 15

Large holding tank capacity
suggested if living aboard
for long periods in area that
requires holding tanks for
both sewage and gray water.
If not, then a 15 gallon plastic
tank can be used.

Sta 27   sta 24

Suggested Holding tanks location, P & S. Toilet
tank to port, gray water from shower to stb.
Tanks can be built in using 1/8" plate, however,
plastic holding tanks are highly suggested for long
term maintenance. Use 1/2" vents.

Similar tank can be installed
in forward cabin for galley
sink gray water.

Use 1 1/2" I.D. minimum fill pipe.
Vents: 3/8" I.D. to 50 gallon, 3/4" for bigger.

DIESEL DUCK
Tank layout
Design by:
George Buehler Yacht Design
P.O. Box 966 Freeland, Whidbey Isl., WA 98249
11/95   1/2" = 1' - 0"

■ **Diesel Duck 38**
plan: tanks

half a million bucks, and many people think there's something
second-rate about a boat that doesn't cost that much, too. Well, sure
you can spend that much on a boat. But you don't really need to. I
don't know why this is so hard for some people to understand.

Here's an example of how building costs break down. The little
Diesel Duck 38 in this chapter has about $7,000 worth of steel in her.
Building her of wood and epoxy would likely cost more, but I don't
know exactly how much more; it depends on how good a shopper
you are (steel, of course, is about the same price anywhere, while lumber prices fluctuate wildly). Add $11,000 for the engine installation
and another 15 to 20 grand to finish her off, and you'll be hard-
pressed to put $35,000 into this boat if you build her yourself.

That's the key, of course: building it yourself. I'm not going to get
into a discussion about boatbuilding here, other than to point out that
lots of people do build their own boats. Many people could never
afford to own a new boat if they didn't build it themselves. Building a
boat isn't quite the big deal many folks think it is. I've done it a couple
of times myself. But there are some popular and nagging misconcep-
tions about boatbuilding, and I'll try to refute them below.

■ *A completed boat looks too complicated to even know where to start.*
Yes, but if you stop and look at the individual parts of the boat
and visualize the steps involved in making them, you'll realize
that most of the work simply involves repetitive basic motor
skills. There's really nothing to it; a boat is simply an assembly of

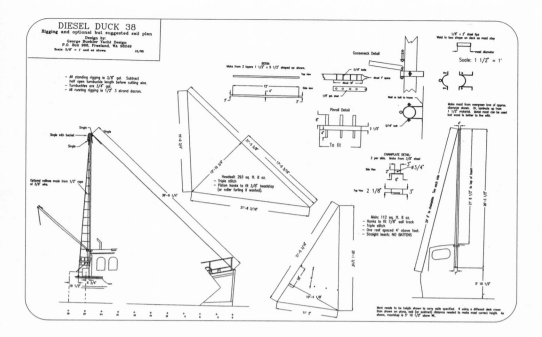

■ **Diesel Duck 38 plan: sail rig detail**

relatively simple parts, each of which is constructed one at a time, and this means you don't need a great skill level to start off.

■ *You need a great deal of cash to start building.* Wrong. You can build most of the boat in increments of several hundred dollars, meaning you can stay busy paycheck to paycheck, paying for materials as you need them. This is perhaps the most appealing part of building your own boat and is how most folks do it. My wife and I built our home this way; it took three years, and there's no mortgage.

■ *You need a big building site.* Wrong again. After you loft it full size on plywood (which you'll later use for the deck or something), practically the whole boat can be prefabricated in the average garage (or even a living room!). Once you have all the frames, deck beams, keel pieces, rudder, and so on cut out and ready, then you can rent a site and throw her together.

I could go on about the personal satisfaction of accomplishing what most folks just dream of doing, but I won't. There is definitely some of that, but don't get me wrong: Building a cruising boat is a lot of work, probably requiring three or more years of serious part-time unsupervised initiative. I've built a couple of boats, but these days I think I'd get the same satisfaction by watching somebody else build my boat.

If you've got a little more money but still have some spare time and the inclination to butcher some wood, the next least expensive way to get a cruising boat is to hire a professional yard to do the steel work and then finish the boat yourself. I say steel in particular because it (or aluminum) goes together faster than other methods, so you'll pay the least in labor. While there probably are still a few really hot wood builders around, not too many yards are left with crews that have the speed we expected as recently as the 1960s.

Prices for hull-only or hull-and-deck construction will depend on how serious the yard is; a small backyard operation has a lower overhead than a big shipyard and so can bid less. The question, of course, is how reputable the backstreet guy is; I wouldn't hire one without references, as well as seeing some of the boats (or at least photos of boats) he's built. And just as with having a house built, you'll want to pay in stages rather than putting the whole amount up front.

As an example of what this approach can cost, in 1997, Custom Steel Boats of North Carolina charged $57,000 for all the steel work in a 38-foot Diesel Duck—that's materials plus 1,300 hours of labor. They did a first-class job, neat and smooth, all seams ground down; tanks, shaft log, and engine bed installed; and included sandblasting and primer paint. The owner had the hull shipped home and will spend another $25,000 or so to finish it out in first-class cruising condition; when he's finished he'll have around $80,000 in the boat. That isn't exactly chump change to most of us, but it isn't an impossible amount either. And it's a lot less than a production boat of similar abilities.

Another cost-effective method is to serve as your own contractor. You rent the building site, buy the materials, hire the labor, and pay them by the hour. The steel work in the Duck 38 might cost around $25,000 done this way, plus sandblasting and priming. If you also hire the carpenters, painters, and mechanics, "subbing" out the whole boat, the cost could get up to $100,000 to $120,000. However, unless you know a bit about all the trades involved, you're running a risk of getting poor work as well as paying too much. One person who built one of my designs this way got seriously took several times down the line. For instance, even the Devco paint factory rep couldn't tell me how a 38-foot boat could eat the 60-odd gallons of their paint that the owner's subcontractor charged him for. If you have no knowledge of the trades involved, you're better off building yourself and learning, or simply buying the whole thing custom-built.

The simplest but most expensive alternative is to get bids from custom shops and order the entire boat built for you. Even here you can save money by getting the yard to agree that you will furnish all the equipment, and you'll just pay them the labor to build the boat and install everything. The prices you'll see will be all over the spectrum, mostly depending on the part of the country where the boat will be built. Yard rates at some struggling places in Maine are under $20 an hour, while here in the Seattle area they're more than $50 an hour. A few years ago a yard in Maine bid $67,000 to build a 38-foot wood Duck, ready to go, less electronics. At the same time, a Seattle yard bid $90,000 just for the steel work.

The point is, if you're considering buying a new production boat, you can easily afford a new custom-built boat even in its most expensive incarnation. And if you can't quite afford a new production boat, you can probably afford some kind of custom boat built to some degree of completion. And if you can't quite afford the down payment on a new production boat, you can still afford to build one yourself.

Troller Yacht Designs

I N THE PAGES THAT FOLLOW you'll find a representative sampling of Troller Yachts. I've designed these boats to be truly practical long-range power cruisers: economical to build, maintain, and run, with efficient interiors. If you compare these study plans with brochures from various production boats, you'll likely think my interiors are very Spartan. Perhaps they are when compared with those production-boat interiors that cram so many bedrooms and closets and toilets into a studio-apartment-size space that there's barely a foot and a half between the bed and the wall and you can't even turn around in the bathroom, but the interiors shown here are designed for *real* life aboard, and they work.

That being said, keep in mind that when you buy a set of plans, you're really paying for the hull lines and mechanical installations. The interior can be laid out however you want; in my experience, most builders change the design several times before they actually finish building the interior.

All these designs have single-chine hulls, which are the quickest and easiest to build, whether in a professional yard or in your own backyard. If you want to build one with a round hull, I'll happily draw it for you, but first, go back to Chapter 7 and look at the three sectional versions of the 57-foot Egis. If you read through the hydrostatics, you'll see that all three have similar numbers. I love round hulls as much as anyone, but I simply see no reason to go to the expense of building one. With single-chine construction, a family of normal means could afford to build and run even a fairly large boat. Frankly, I just can't accept that a 40-foot boat has to cost $400,000. Still, the choice is yours.

All these boats share a certain family resemblance, mostly because they are all designed to perform the same job: cruise long distances under power, safely and economically. Most are flush decked aft, for example, because the aft deck is the best place to carry a decent skiff, and cruising without a decent skiff is a drag. All have backup sail rigs, because this is the safest way to cruise. I just sold a motorcycle that would hit 80 in second gear, and it still had three more gears left, so that should tell you that I'm a fairly reckless guy. But no way would I ever venture very far from land in a motorboat not equipped with backup sails. I mean, that's *reckless*.

Most of these boats are a bit chunkier than the troller *Frances* that we met in Chapter 3. To me, *Frances* is about the sexiest boat in the world, and one of the finest seaboats you'll ever see for her length. But there's simply no room in her, and since a cruising boat must also be a comfortable place to live, the smaller designs were necessarily compromises. Drawing them big enough for their length to have a comfortable interior didn't hurt their seagoing abilities, and if you compare them to the typical trawler yacht they're still quite sleek. They ain't *Frances,* but then a surf boat ain't a kayak, either, and that isn't criticism. Well, come to the think of it, Ellemaid really is *Frances,* and someday I'm going to own her, although lately I've been leaning toward the stripped-down Wunderburg version. But recently Egis has started growing on me big time, and I'm thinking she'd be the perfect boat to go back to Iceland and do some serious cruising, but then so would the 48-foot Duck. Or maybe I'd be smarter to spend four months nailing up simple little Pilgrim and then head south for a bit. Maybe . . . .

DIESEL DUCK 38

THE DUCKS WERE DESIGNED to combine the Troller Yacht philosophy with a hull shape that can be built of steel as quickly and inexpensively as a seaworthy displacement hull can be. Their hull lines are so smooth, the steel just flows around, and the finished hull looks as smooth as plywood, without using any bondo or fillers.

Diesel Duck 38's complete plans were shown in Chapter 11, but I want to discuss her a bit here. This is about the shortest a voyaging powerboat can be, if the two adults she's intended for aren't to come to blows after an extended time at sea. Because she's short she needs to be full bodied, sort of like what the personal ads call a "BBW" (Big Beautiful Woman), giving her a D/L of 313. It would be possible to build her a foot or two shorter, but what's the point? You'll save next to nothing in building costs (outfitting and power would be identical) and have even less room aboard.

Much of the credit for the original design, the *Patti Ann*, goes to Pat Blackshaw. Pat and her husband, Joe, were longtime liveaboards but were fed up with sailboats in general and the handling, structural, and mechanical problems of their 45-foot imported sailboat in particular. They had reached retirement age, and the siren call of traveling in straight lines in a snug, heated wheelhouse proved irresistible. To the shock of their sailing friends, they decided to go for a power cruiser. Not finding any production boats that really fit their needs and not willing to buy an older custom boat and risk inheriting a whole new set of problems, they decided a new custom boat was their best answer and hired me to design it.

LOD: 38' 3"
LWL: 36' 4"
Beam: 12' 9"
Draft: 4' 9"
Displ.: 32,669 lbs
Power: 28-hp Gardner or 30-hp SABB suggested; 50- to 80-hp okay too.

PROJECTED SPEED/POWER REQUIREMENTS, CALM AND OFF-WEATHER CONDITIONS

V/L	SPEED (KNOTS)	HORSEPOWER	RANGE WITH 600 GALLONS @ .06 GAL/HP HOUR (MILES)
1	6.13	5.2	11,788
1.1	6.63	6.8	9,750
1.2	7.23	12.8	5,648
1.25	7.53	17.2	4,378
1.3	7.84	23.3	3,365
1.35	8.14	31.6	2,576

Pat and I fought tooth and nail during the preliminary design sketches, but she held me to her requirement of staying under 40 feet. I like to stretch out hulls rather than try to squeeze a livable interior into a small space, but by the late 1980s, big-city marina rates in California were running $11 to $14 per foot a month, and Pat refused

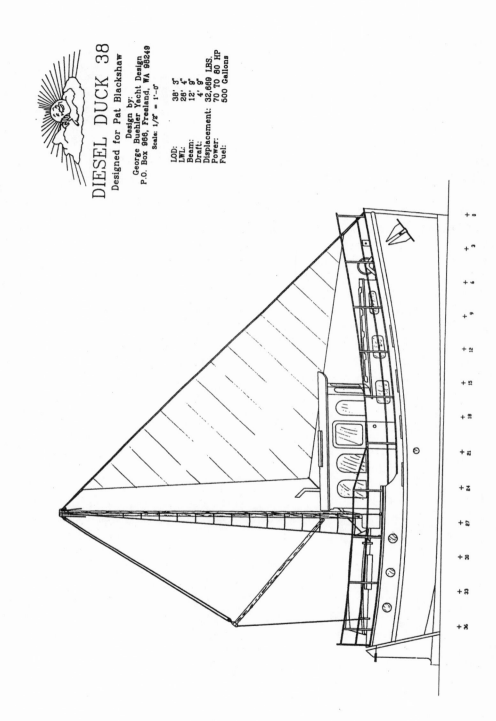

DIESEL DUCK 38

Designed for Pat Blackshaw

Design by:
George Buehler Yacht Design
P.O. Box 966, Freeland, WA 98249

Scale: 1/2" = 1'-0"

LOD: 38' 3"
LWL: 28' 4"
Beam: 12' 9"
Draft: 4' 9"
Displacement: 32,669 LBS.
Power: 70 TO 80 HP
Fuel: 500 Gallons

to let me talk her into a longer boat. And she was right. By keeping the emphasis solely on the comforts of the owners (and not guests), and by making the hull rather "big" for its length (although not by trawler-yacht standards), we were able to fit in a functional liveaboard interior.

This is how custom design is supposed to work, by the way, with a client's strong ideas and very specific needs leavening the designer's preconceived notions. Neither of us could have come up with this design alone. I drew and Pat rejected all sorts of versions before we arrived at the final result you see here. This boat has worked out great, and much of the credit is due to Pat's tenacity, vision, and plain mule stubbornness.

The original was built of steel by Don and Jeff Millereck at Coast Marine Construction, in Cotati, California. Unfortunately, soon after construction started, Joe died, but Pat had the boat finished and lived aboard for several years in Oakland, California, cruising locally and once down the coast to San Diego. After several years of living aboard and looking for crew that could take off whenever Pat felt like going, she sold the boat in 1996. The last I heard the new owner had cruised down to Mexico.

This boat's friendly, rugged good looks have made her very appealing to serious cruisers. She's a heavy craft, a good seaboat, she's comfortable for extended stays aboard, and has the range to travel wherever you want to go.

LOD: 44'
LWL: 41' 9"
Beam: 14'
Draft: 5'
Displ.: 45,160 lbs
Power: 72-hp
Deere or equal

ALTHOUGH THE 38-FOOTER WORKS FINE for two people, she's still just a bit cramped. A number of folks asked for a version stretched to fit in a guest cabin or office area, and here's the result. This boat has the same profile as the 38 but is a bit wider. From the transom to the front of the wheelhouse, she follows the same layout as the 38; the stern owner's cabin, the engine room, and the wheelhouse are sufficiently comfortable on the 38, and I saw no reason to enlarge them. Only the front half has been extended, and now there's room for a guest cabin in the bow, along with a larger bathroom and a more spread-out living area.

It will cost very little more to build the 44, and most of that will be a little more steel. The expensive things—the engine and running gear, steering gear, anchoring system, even the material scantlings, are almost identical. Unless I had a very specific reason to build the smaller boat, such as owning a slip the 44-footer wouldn't fit, I'd go with the 44. With boats, bigger is almost always better, although as you'll see, the extra displacement raises the 44's operational costs a bit.

	PROJECTED SPEED/POWER REQUIREMENTS, CALM AND OFF-WEATHER CONDITIONS		
V/L	**SPEED (KNOTS)**	**HORSEPOWER**	**RANGE WITH 700 GALLONS @ .06 GAL/HP HOUR (MILES)**
1	6.46	7.8	11,667
1.1	7.11	11.9	6,970
1.2	7.76	19.0	4,795
1.25	8.08	25.4	3,711
1.3	8.4	34.5	2,841
1.35	8.73	46.9	2,172

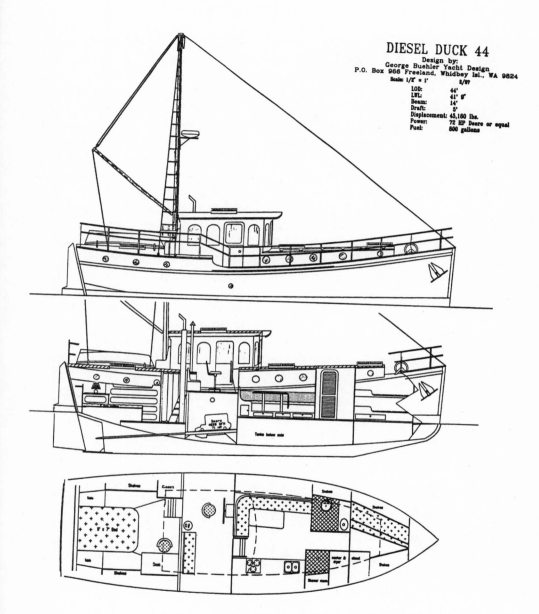

DIESEL DUCK 44

Design by:
George Buehler Yacht Design
P.O. Box 966 Freeland, Whidbey Isl., WA 9824

Scale: 1/2" = 1'   2/87

LOD: 44'
LWL: 41' 8"
Beam: 14'
Draft: 5'
Displacement: 45,160 lbs.
Power: 72 HP Deere or equal
Fuel: 600 gallons

LOD: 48'
LWL: 45' 10"
Beam: 14' 1"
Draft: 5' 6"
Displ.: 50,613 lbs
Power: 71- to
100-hp Deere
or equal

NOW WE'RE GETTING INTO THE RANGE of a spacious cruising home. The 48's a substantial boat, but she's also the trimmest of the Duck family, carrying the same beam as the 44, with the extra length spread throughout the design. The owner's cabin, engine room, and wheelhouse are a little longer than those on the 38 and 44. The forward cabin and guest cabin/office area are more spacious. She has a real bathroom with a nice bathtub. She's entirely flush decked to provide the maximum feeling of spaciousness below decks as well as make her even easier to build. The flush deck drops down to the main sheer along each side of the wheelhouse and in the very bow by the windlass, breaking up the deck line and making things more visually interesting as well as giving you more of a feeling of being *in* the boat rather than on it. There's a heavy railing made of 1 1/2-inch pipe welded to the deck so you'll feel secure anywhere aboard.

While all the Ducks have a rugged and businesslike air, I like the strong good looks of this guy the best. As you head out of the jetty mouth, you'll engage the autopilot, then climb the ladder to the fly bridge and settle down into the bridge seat, sipping your drink and smelling the salt air and listening to the faint throb of the diesel dry stack. As you survey the sea and the retreating coastline, you'll feel like Seaman First Class Wolf Steiner himself, piloting *Der Bismarck,* or maybe Mother Foss, the foundress of the great Foss Tug & Barge Company.

	PROJECTED SPEED/POWER REQUIREMENTS, CALM AND OFF-WEATHER CONDITIONS		
V/L	SPEED (KNOTS)	HORSEPOWER	RANGE WITH 900 GALLONS @ .06 GAL/HP HOUR (MILES)
1	6.77	8.9	11,410
1.1	7.44	13.7	8,146
1.2	8.12	21.8	5,587
1.25	8.46	29.2	4,346
1.3	8.8	39.7	3,298
1.35	9.14	53.9	2,544

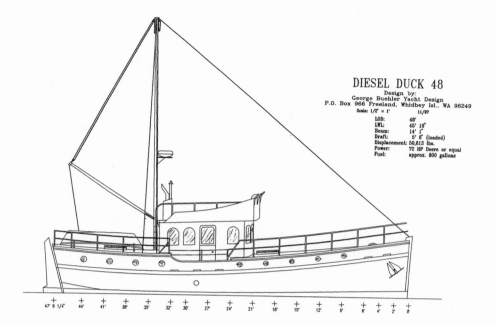

DIESEL DUCK 48

Design by:
George Buehler Yacht Design
P.O. Box 966 Freeland, Whidbey Isl., WA 98249

Scale: 1/2" = 1'   11/97

LOD:	48'
LWL:	45' 10"
Beam:	14' 1"
Draft:	5' 6" (loaded)
Displacement:	50,613 lbs.
Power:	72 HP Deere or equal
Fuel:	approx. 800 gallons

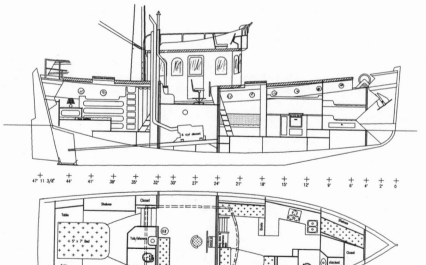

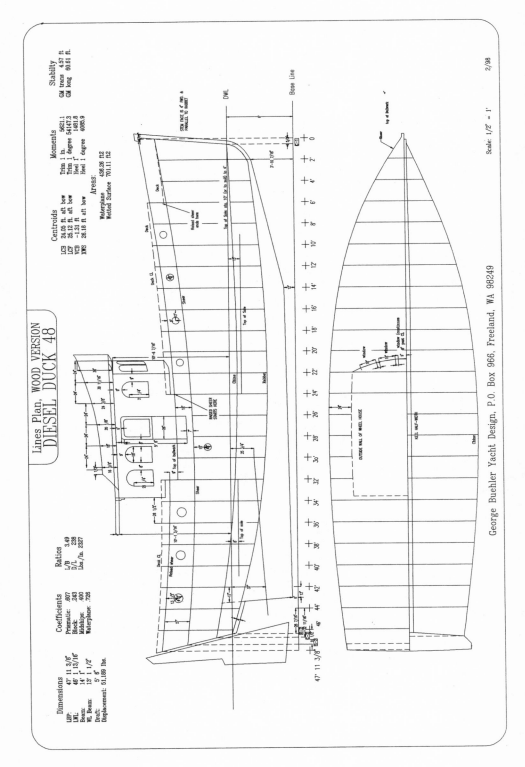

Lines Plan, WOOD VERSION
DIESEL DUCK 48

Dimensions
LBP: 47' 11 3/8"
LWL: 46' 1 13/16"
Beam: 14' 1"
WL Beam: 13' 1 1/2"
Draft: 5' 8"
Displacement: 51,189 lbs.

Coefficients
Prismatic: .607
Block: .243
Midships: .400
Waterplane: .728

Ratios
L/B 3.49
D/L 238
Lbs./In. 2327

Centroids
LCB 24.05 ft. aft. bow
LCF 25.12 ft. aft. bow
VCB -1.31 ft.
XWS 26.18 ft. aft. bow

Moments
Trim 1 in. 5621.1
Trim 1 degree 54147.3
Heel 1° 1481.8
Heel 1 degree 4085.9

Areas:
Waterplane 436.26 ft2
Wetted Surface 701.11 ft2

Stability
GM trans 4.57 ft.
GM long 60.61 ft.

George Buehler Yacht Design, P.O. Box 966, Freeland, WA 98249

Scale: 1/2" = 1'

2/98

ALCINA 48

I'M PARTIAL TO DOUBLE-ENDERS and wood hulls, although there's no logic to it. Transom hulls like the Ducks, where the beam at the transom is high and the hull is actually double-ended at the waterline, are just as seaworthy in all conditions except running backward in the surf. They have more interior volume and deck space back aft, and they're easier to build than double-enders, since you don't have to wrap the hull material around as much of a curve. I know all that, but I don't care. I just prefer the look of double-ended hulls.

Alcina is a heavy-duty boat, but she doesn't push the limits of a Troller Yacht. She's set up for two people's long-term comfort, but of course the interior can be changed around anyway you want. The Duck 44's interior would fit in okay, at the expense of the spaciousness of this interior. For example, as drawn she has an 8-foot engine room; and the Duck 44 has just 6 feet. Two feet doesn't sound like much, but in practice it is. Personally, I wouldn't trade a large engine room with space for a good workbench and lots of storage and even a generator if you feel like it just for some guest beds. You can always make a dinette so it drops down to form a guest bed. This works fine, and your guests won't be so comfortable that they move in.

The house's sloped front and back walls seemed *right* to me at the time I drew this boat, and I still like the look, but of course this complicates construction a little, and the boat will work just fine with vertical walls. Actually, the back wall is vertical, as you'll see on the interior drawing, but the side walls are angled so that they form sides for a big seat nested against the back wall of the house. This seat also serves as a deck box, with the propane tanks, fenders, and dock lines stored inside.

Alcina certainly could be built of steel, but as drawn she's a wood boat. Since she's a big one, the construction plan calls for a good deal of epoxy lamination. It's hard to get decent-size wood of any quality these days, and it's very expensive when you do. Laminated pieces are lighter and needn't be of the same quality; the keel and stems, for example, are laminated from construction-grade "2-by" material from the lumberyard. The hull planking is one layer of lumberyard 1 × 4 (3/4- × 3 1/2-inch finished) covered with three layers of 3/8-inch plywood, or one layer of 2 × 4 (1 1/2- × 3 1/2-inch finished) covered with two layers of 3/8-inch plywood topped with a layer of glass cloth and epoxy resin. Of course she can also be single-planked with 2-inch wood. That's the traditional way to do it, but there's a lot to be said for the composite-planking approach: It's absolutely leakproof, almost bulletproof, and easy to do yourself, and it leaves you with a boat requiring about the least maintenance of any material while having all

LOD: 47' 6"
LWL: 45' 10"
Beam: 14' 1"
Draft: 5' 9"
Displ.: 54,643 lbs
Power: 71- to
100-hp Deere
or equal

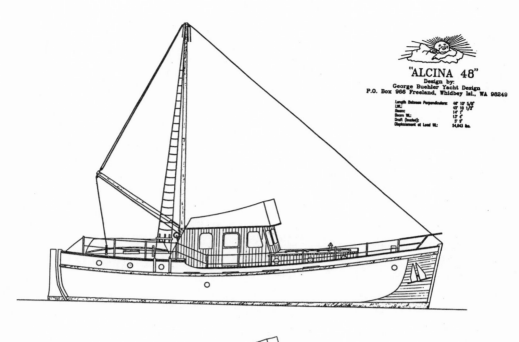

"ALCINA 48"
Design by:
George Buehler Yacht Design
P.O. Box 966 Freeland, Whidbey Isl., WA 98249

Length Between Perpendiculars:	48' 10' 5/8"
LWL:	45' 19 1/2'
Beam:	14' 6'
Beam WL:	13' 6'
Draft (loaded):	5' 6'
Displacement at Load WL:	54,943 lbs.

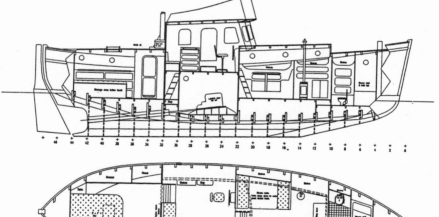

Interior Plan
"ALCINA 48"
Design by:
George Buehler Yacht Design
P.O. Box 966 Freeland, Whidbey Isl., WA 98249
Scale 1/2" = 1'   4/92

the advantages of wood construction—sound dampening, natural insulation, psychological warmth, and ease of building-in things. The only thing I don't like about composite construction is the lack of caulking seams. I *love* looking at a wood hull with caulking seams. Some people route in phony seams, just as some plastic boats have seams molded in. To me that's crass; don't do it on *my* designs.

I gave Alcina an outboard rudder because I like the look, and no matter what the rest of my profession says, I think that extra couple of feet in the water increases the effective waterline length without increasing the displacement, thereby increasing hull speed without increasing power needs. But just to be conservative, I didn't figure in the extra length of the outboard rudder when I made the power/speed predictions. Still, we found with the 38-foot Duck that *something* makes them move faster with less fuel than the books say they should. My money's on the outboard rudder.

	PROJECTED SPEED/POWER REQUIREMENTS, CALM AND OFF-WEATHER CONDITIONS		
V/L	SPEED (KNOTS)	HORSEPOWER	RANGE WITH 800 GALLONS @ .06 GAL/HP HOUR (MILES)
1	6.77	10.0	9,027
1.1	7.44	13.7	7,241
1.2	8.12	21.8	4,966
1.25	8.46	29.2	3,863
1.3	8.8	39.7	2,955
1.35	9.14	53.9	2,261

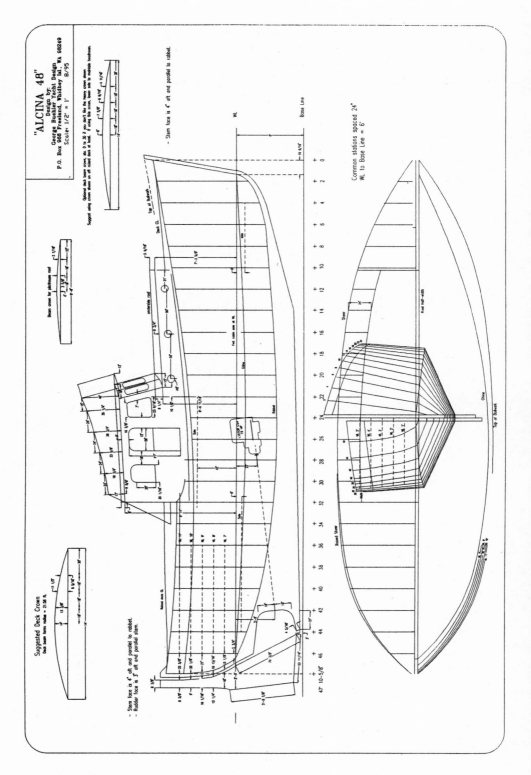

"ALCINA 48"
Design by:
George Buehler Yacht Design
P.O. Box 966 Freeland, Whidbey Isl, WA 98249
Scale: 1/2" = 1'
8/95

THIS DESIGN IS ONE OF MY FAVORITES, a Troller Yacht in the *Frances* tradition. She's long enough to have an extremely comfortable interior while the hull remains unusually trim and slippery. Her D/L is only 167, but she's still a hefty boat, solidly welded up from ¼- and 5/16-inch plate.

Back in 1980 I spent a few months in Iceland, then went on and poked around some of the Norwegian fjords as well as I could by car. I've always wanted to go back by boat, and I think this is the boat I'd like to do it in. She's easily driven, very livable, should be seaworthy as hell, and best of all she just looks right.

The indicated power is a 4-71 Jimmy, which at 115 continuous horsepower is far more engine than needed. But as I worked up this design, I kept thinking about high-latitude cruising, pushing against currents, making frequent short hops at close to hull speed so as to arrive at the next harbor before dark (entering a strange place at night is the single most dangerous thing you can do when cruising); because rebuilt 4-71s are inexpensive and easy to find, and the extra power would come in handy in the far north or south, I drew one in.

LOD: 57' 3"
LWL: 53' 11"
Beam: 14' 4"
Draft: 6'
Displ.: Chine hull
  56,645 lbs
  Round hull
  61,734 lbs
Power: To suit;
  3-71 GMC or
  equal; 4-71
  okay

PROJECTED SPEED/POWER REQUIREMENTS, CALM AND OFF-WEATHER CONDITIONS, CHINE VERSION

V/L	SPEED (KNOTS)	HORSEPOWER	RANGE WITH 900 GALLONS @ .06 GAL/HP HOUR (MILES)
1	7.34	11.2	9,830
1.1	8.07	17.3	6,997
1.2	8.80	27.5	4,800
1.25	9.17	36.9	3,728
1.3	9.54	50	2,862
1.35	9.91	68	2,186

This boat needs only somewhere around 30 to 40 horsepower in normal cruising, which may be too light a continuous load for a 4-71; that's a question for the dealer. If your cruising plans don't include a lot of man-against-the-sea stuff, a 3-71 would be a better choice; it's rated for a continuous 82 horsepower and so would be happy running at half of that or less.

The profile drawing shows an outboard rudder, and this is how I'd build it. The interior view shows a normal inboard rudder, however, so it's your choice.

I worked up the lines for both round-bottom and chine hulls just to show how they compare. If I win the lottery I might at least think about having the round-bottom version with reverse-curve garboards

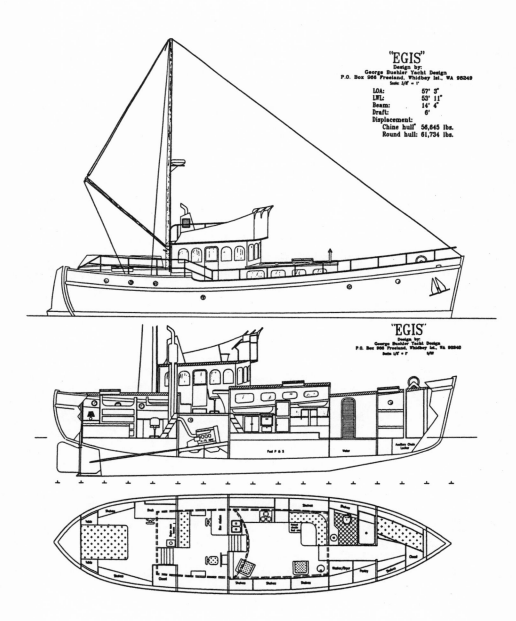

"EGIS"
Design by:
George Buehler Yacht Design
P.O. Box 966 Freeland, Whidbey Isl., WA 98249
Scale: 3/8" = 1'

LOA:	57' 3"
LWL:	53' 11"
Beam:	14' 4"
Draft:	6'
Displacement:	
Chine hull	56,645 lbs.
Round hull:	61,734 lbs.

"EGIS"
Design by:
George Buehler Yacht Design
P.O. Box 966 Freeland, Whidbey Isl., WA 98249
Scale 1/8" = 1'

built, just 'cause it looks so pretty hauled out. In the end, though, I'd probably go with the brute strength and reef resistance of a heavy steel hull, and round-bilge steel construction doesn't provide enough benefits to justify its extra expense over a single-chine boat. Besides, a single-chine double-ender with its chine line underwater looks pretty good afloat; you'd be hard-pressed to tell the difference. Years ago, I remember a very attractive lady admiring a sailboat I owned. Naturally I invited her aboard for a cup of tea. She really liked old *Juno,* and as we talked she mentioned how much she disliked chine hulls and how full of crap that guy Buehler was. We had a good visit, and as she was leaving I couldn't resist telling her that she'd been admiring a chine boat, and I happened to be that guy Buehler! She had a good sense of humor, and we became friends.

LOD: 70' 8"
LWL: 66' 10"
Beam: 14' 2"
Draft: 5' 6"
Displ.: 72,000 lbs
Power: 72 to 100
hp

IHAD A LOT OF FUN WITH THIS DESIGN, the idea being a simple and inexpensive boat that would be super comfortable for a couple (or two couples, or a couple with kids) and highly fuel efficient to do some serious traveling.

I love the profile. I got the idea from a British magazine that featured the work of a Swedish powerboat designer. One photo showed a 40-footer heading out into a fairly rough sea, and I thought it really looked slick. Hence Wunderburg, which is much longer, with single-chine steel construction, a V-drive, sail assist, and an orgy-size bedroom (Wunderburg being the town in old German legend where the Wild Women lived).

If I were planning to operate this boat primarily in lousy weather, I'd likely add some sort of small pilothouse. But in more benign environments, this open cockpit would work well, and you'd still be more comfortable than the average cruising sailboat owner sitting outside steering with a stick, especially if you added an automotive-type heater next to the steering wheel. I based this cockpit design on my old Chris-Craft Sea Skiff, which has a folding canvas top and side curtains to keep out the weather; I use this boat comfortably pretty much year-round. If the cockpit got too uncomfortable, just hook in the autopilot, set a 2-mile alarm on the radar, and keep watch below.

PROJECTED SPEED/POWER REQUIREMENTS, CALM AND OFF-WEATHER CONDITIONS

V/L	SPEED (KNOTS)	HORSEPOWER	RANGE WITH **800** GALLONS @ .06 GAL/HP HOUR (MILES)
1	8.14	15.3	7,084
1.1	8.95	23.6	5,056
1.2	9.76	37.6	3,461
1.25	10.17	50.3	2,696
1.3	10.58	68.3	2,065
1.35	10.98	92.8	1,578

This would be a great boat for warm climates. Imagine the decks covered with windsurfers and kayaks and people wearing swimsuits. Imagine traveling between the Islands (and to them, for that matter) at 10 knots, burning just over 2 gallons an hour in a ship this size. With its long, narrow hull, not much would slow it down. My neighbor Fred has an old boat, 72 × 12 feet, that slips along at 10 knots no matter what he's going into.

Because this boat moves so easily and has so little windage, it doesn't need much power, so I've drawn in a 71-horsepower (53 continuous)

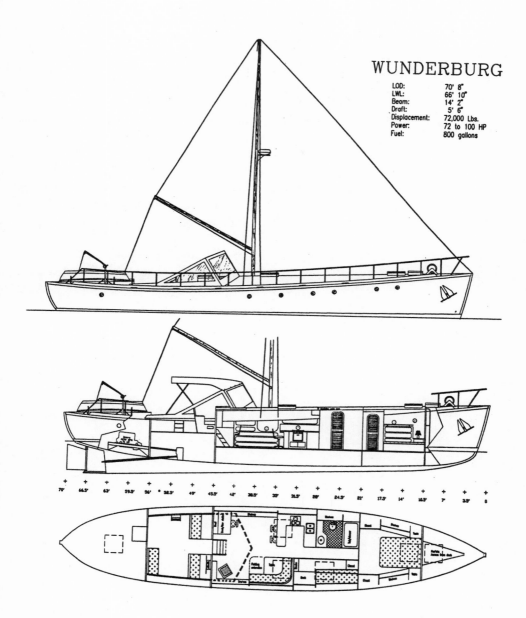

WUNDERBURG

LOD:	70' 8"
LWL:	66' 10"
Beam:	14' 2"
Draft:	5' 6"
Displacement:	72,000 Lbs.
Power:	72 to 100 HP
Fuel:	800 gallons

Deere. That sounds pretty small for a boat this size, but the numbers say it will be plenty. Of course, if you want more speed there's no reason you couldn't install a bigger engine; she should hit 11 knots with 93 horsepower, and that's pretty fast. I think I'd be perfectly happy cruising at 9 1/2 knots at 1 5/8 gallons per hour, myself. To get that extra 1 1/2 knots, you'd burn 3.8 gallons more fuel, or a little over 5 1/2 gallons per hour. Of course that's still pretty economical for a boat this size, but it's the principal of the thing. To make more room, I stuck the engine clear back in the stern, using a V-drive and a wet exhaust (no place for a dry stack); you'd hardly know the engine was there.

The interior should be very comfortable. There's a huge owner's cabin, a bathroom with a tub, a galley with stools and a breakfast counter, and a good-size living room with a big desk. The guest cabin has bunk beds. You could stick a guest double in there, if you pushed the cabin out into the corridor. That would take out the tub, however, and no way would I trade a bathtub for a double bed for occasional guests. It's up to you, though.

ELLEMAID 81

THIS HULL REMINDS ME of the lovely New England sardine carriers, boats that were every bit as able and attractive as the West Coast salmon trollers. Most people design or build something, from a dress or a garden to a birdhouse or a boat, because it makes us feel good. And this hull, well . . . it turns me on.

Ellemaid (what the Swedes called their Wild Women) is essentially Wunderburg's basic idea but stretched 10 feet and drawn a little less radical and made more comfortable for full-time liveaboards. There's a big wheelhouse, because aside from the novelty of traveling in straight lines at a consistent speed, a big part of the cruising powerboat's appeal is that big, comfortable wheelhouse, where you can sit at the helm, warm and dry and wearing slippers, and lean back and look out the windows as the heater keeps things at 75°F and the windshield wipers flip back and forth.

The best comparison between the behavior of a boat like this and a typical trawler-style hull came from a crab-boat captain friend of mine. He was plowing across the Bering Sea in a storm, the 110-foot tank-of-a-crab boat (a crab boat's fat hull is essentially similar to many contemporary trawler yachts) standing on its head and barely making headway. Behind him, way back on the horizon, he saw a speck. Pretty soon the speck turned into a boat. Soon after that the boat drew alongside and then passed him; it was one of those wonderful old halibut schooners. These "schooners" (they're primarily powerboats, not sailboats; see Chapter 1) are like Super Trollers, ranging from maybe 60 to 80 feet or so, shaped very much like Ellemaid, but deeper and heav-

LOD: 81'	
LWL: 76' 5"	
Beam: 14' 1"	
Draft: 6' 6"	
Displ.: 100,924 lbs	
Power: 100 to 150 hp	

	PROJECTED SPEED/POWER REQUIREMENTS, CALM AND OFF-WEATHER CONDITIONS		
V/L	**SPEED (KNOTS)**	**HORSEPOWER**	**RANGE WITH 1000 GALLONS @ .06 GAL/HP HOUR (MILES)**
1	8.75	23.5	11,170
1.1	9.62	36.1	7,994
1.2	10.5	57.4	5,489
1.25	10.93	76.9	4,264
1.3	11.37	104.4	3,267
1.35	11.81	141.9	2,497
1.5	13.12	388.4	306 *This one's just for fun*

ier. Bill said it was rolling and pitching in the rough seas but was maintaining speed, and it left him in its wake.

Her 81-foot length might make you think this is a damn big boat, but it isn't: *length* doesn't make a boat big; *hull volume* makes a boat

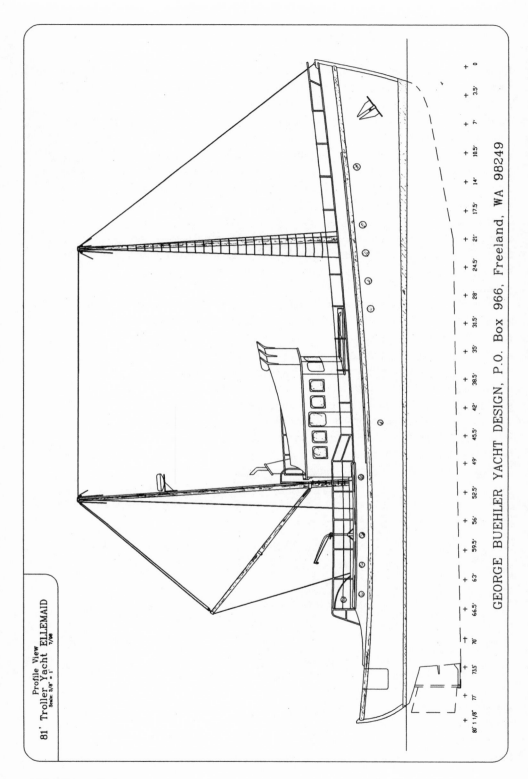

Profile View
81' Troller Yacht ELLEMAID
Scale: 3/8" = 1'
7/98

GEORGE BUEHLER YACHT DESIGN, P.O. Box 966, Freeland, WA 98249

big. It doesn't matter whether you put X cubic feet in a short, fat, deep package or in a long, narrow, shallow package, it's still X cubic feet. But a stretched-out hull is easier to build (fewer radical curves), the hull goes through the water easier, and you get a more spacious interior. Building and outfitting costs between short and fat and long and lean will be almost identical (adding a bit for extra interior work), because there is still X volume. You'll pay more for dock space, but if you're building a boat for cruising, then moorage costs are far less important than cruising qualities. And here the long, lean boat excels.

Look at the deck space! With solid welded pipe railing on the raised deck aft of the wheelhouse, 28-inch-wide side decks at the house, and 18-inch solid bulwarks with a 32-inch-high railing from amidships running to the bow, you can jog aboard if you want. There's even a deep cockpit in the stern with a fighting chair and a small freezer hold.

Ellemaid may be an 81-footer, but she's a *small* 81-footer, with a D/L of only 101. That long length makes possible an extremely comfortable interior, however. The interior drawing seems to show a lot of white space, but you get to appreciate all this elbow room when living aboard. The private stern cabin is 20 feet long, with a 5- × 7-foot bed (which all these designs have, except Pilgrim), a full bathroom with a real bathtub, a closet and dresser and lots of shelves, and a 7-foot office-size desk—big enough for real projects without having to pick up for meals or company. For instance, my wife, a hell of a seamstress, could have her 1930s Singer built into a desk like this and there'd still be room for my word processor.

The wheelhouse floor is 11 1/2 feet long, and there's a big steering station, a lounge with table, a permanent chart desk with storage drawers, lots more elbow room, and lots of big windows. The forward cabin is very spacious, thanks in part to the flush-deck design. There's a huge galley, a second bathroom, and a large guest cabin forward.

This guest cabin has possibilities beyond being a repository for visitors. Modern communications—fax machines, air express, satellite phones, E-mail—have opened up all sorts of new ways to earn a living without leaving home. There are five AutoCad developers just on the south end of the island where we live; God knows how many other programmers, freelance writers, consultants, and so on live back in the trees. My last boat was bought by a guy who used it for more than 10 years as a traveling doctor's office serving isolated Alaska communities. This boat's forward cabin would be ideal for that, or it would make a great dentist's office, photo lab, programmer's office, or especially an electronics repair shop. There's a fortune to be made fixing and maintaining the elaborate electronic and mechanical systems installed on so many modern yachts. When you enter a port, just stick up a sign advertising your skills, and you'll have all the business you can handle.

I drew in a 4-71 for the same reasons I gave for Egis, but you'll rarely if ever need that much power, and a 3-71 would be just fine. Actually, since the engine room is 11 feet long, if it were my boat I'd at least think about putting in a Gardner. If you wanted one badly enough, you could power over to England with a 3-71 and swap it out for a Gardner, although this would only be worth doing if you were truly engine crazy.

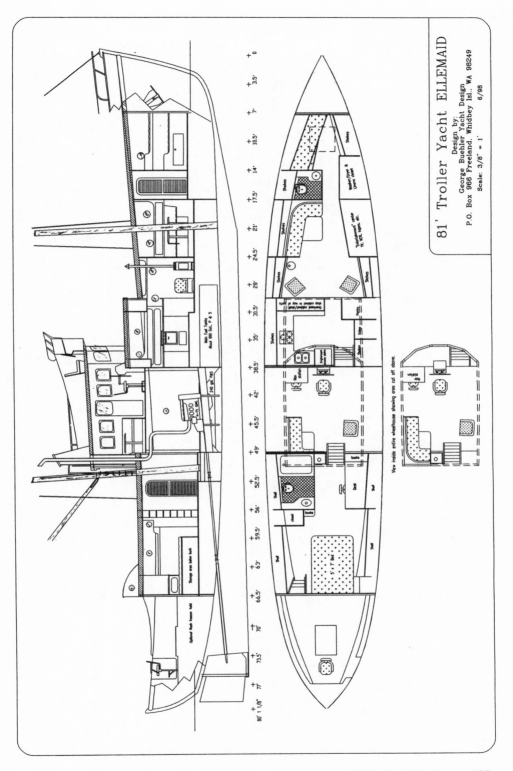

81' Troller Yacht ELLEMAID

Design by:
George Buehler Yacht Design.
P.O. Box 966 Freeland. Whidbey Isl.. WA 98249
Scale: 3/8" = 1'   6/98

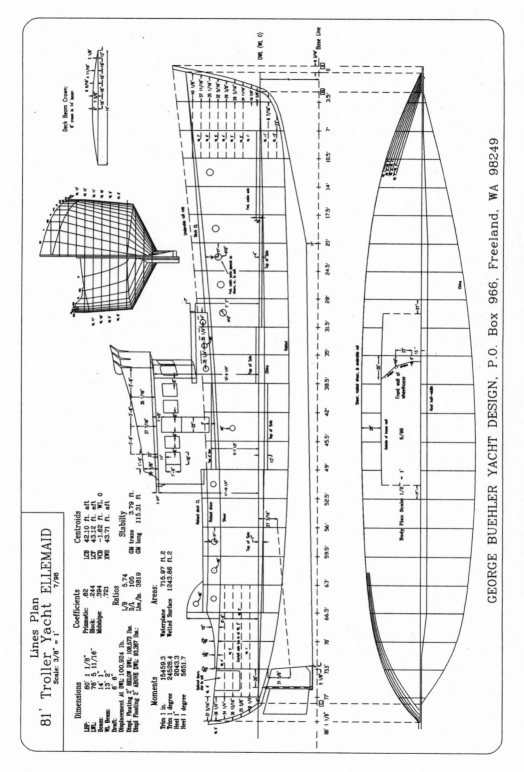

Lines Plan
81' Troller Yacht ELLEMAID
Scale: 3/8" = 1'   7/98

Dimensions
LBP: 80' 1 1/8"
LWL: 76' 5 11/16"
Beam: 14' 1'
WL Beam: 13' 2"
Draft: 6' 6"
Displacement At DWL: 100,824 lb.
Displ. Floating 2" BELOW DWL: 108,673 lbs.
Displ. Floating 2" ABOVE DWL: 93,387 lbs.

Coefficients
Prismatic: .62
Block: .244
Midships: .721

Ratios
L/B 5.74
D/L 105
Lbs./In. 3819

Centroids
LCB 42.10 ft. aft
LCF 43.12 ft. aft
VCB -1.62 ft. WL 0
XWS 43.71 ft. aft

Stability
GM trans 3.79 ft.
GM long 115.31 ft.

Areas:
Waterplane 715.97 ft.2
Wetted Surface 1243.86 ft.2

Moments
Trim 1 in. 15459.3
Trim 1 degree 24528.4
Heel 1 degree 20043.3
Heel 1 degree 5651.7

GEORGE BUEHLER YACHT DESIGN, P.O. Box 966, Freeland, WA 98249

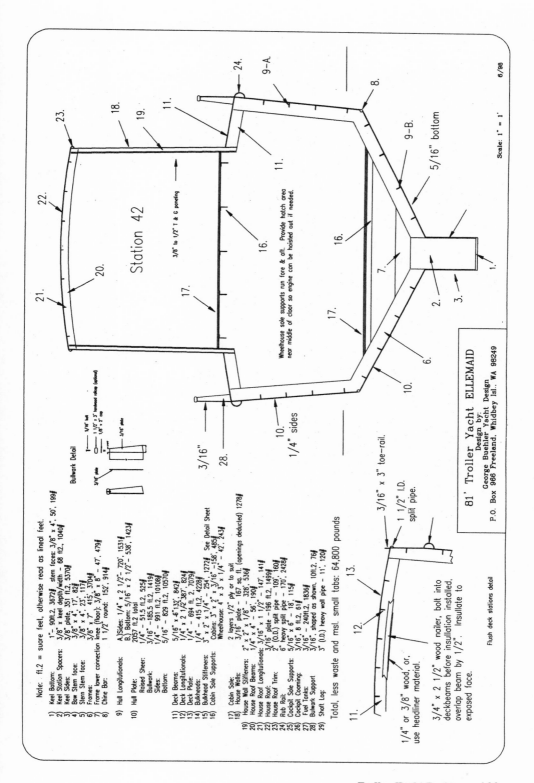

LOD: 44' 11"
LWL: 40' 7"
Beam: 10' 6"
Draft: 3' 4"
Displ.: 10,941 lbs
Displ. loaded 3"
past LWL:
13,158 lbs
Power: 10-hp
Sabb or other
small, slow-
turning diesel

WHO EVER HEARD of a long-range cruising powerboat within financial range of a burger flipper? Well, why the hell not? It's about the only everyday-folks job our economy's creating anymore.

Pilgrim is designed for singlehanding or for a very friendly couple, and will be extremely simple, fast, and cheap to build; I don't see 15,000 1998 dollars in her, including the new 10-horse Sabb diesel, or more than six months building time. She's built of plywood and lumberyard stuff. There's only one bunk, but on a passage a couple would trade watches, and in port the dinette table can be easily and quickly converted to a double at night.

Pilgrim has an open cockpit with a speedboat-type folding canvas top. This boat is so low and light that, as much as I tried, I simply couldn't come up with an enclosed wheelhouse that didn't make her look top-heavy. This cockpit is similar to my Chris-Craft's, and is far better than sitting in the cockpit of some sailboat. And if you had the water-cooled Sabb, you could always stick an automotive-type heater at about foot level (and you might be able to duct some heat off the air-cooled Lister with a fan).

			RANGE WITH **100** GALLONS @
V/L	**SPEED (KNOTS)**	**HORSEPOWER**	**.06 GAL/HP HOUR (MILES)**
1	5.89	1.4	7,012
1.1	6.48	2.2	4,909
1.2	7.07	3.4	3,466
1.25	7.36	4.6	2,667
1.3	7.66	6.3	2,026
1.35	7.95	8.5	1,559

PROJECTED SPEED/POWER REQUIREMENTS, CALM AND OFF-WEATHER CONDITIONS

As small as she is, Pilgrim's still a real cruising boat and so needs to carry a decent skiff. The back third is flush decked to carry the skiff, with the large space below available for storage.

This is kind of a weird little boat, but she should be lots of fun for very little money. Her light displacement and minimal room mean she carries only 100 gallons of diesel, but that still gives her a pretty good range. And there's a backup sail plan, so you'll never get stuck. While Pilgrim certainly has the ability to cross oceans, I think I'd use it for coasting instead; I'd be a bit uncomfortable heading off soundings in something this light, not to mention you'd be running the fuel down fairly low before you reach the next continent. Of course you can always carry a few extra 5-gallon containers of diesel for a long trip.

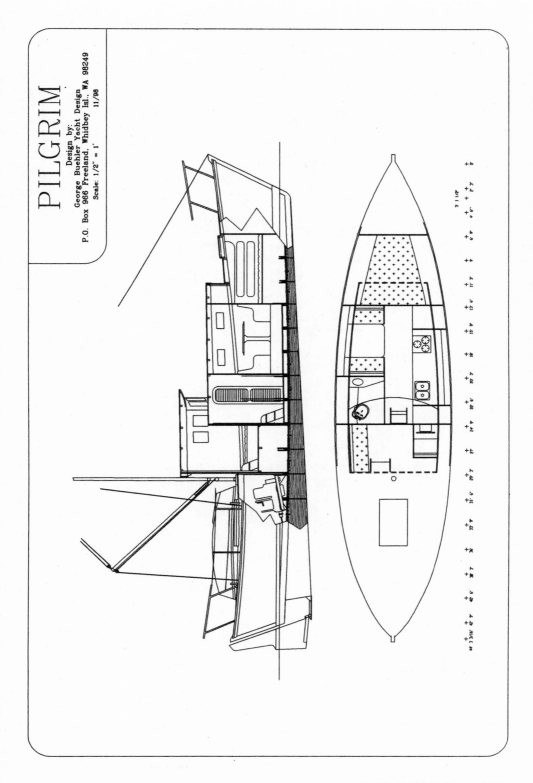

PILGRIM

Design by:
George Buehler Yacht Design
P.O. Box 966 Freeland, Whidbey Isl., WA 98249
Scale: 1/2" = 1'   11/98

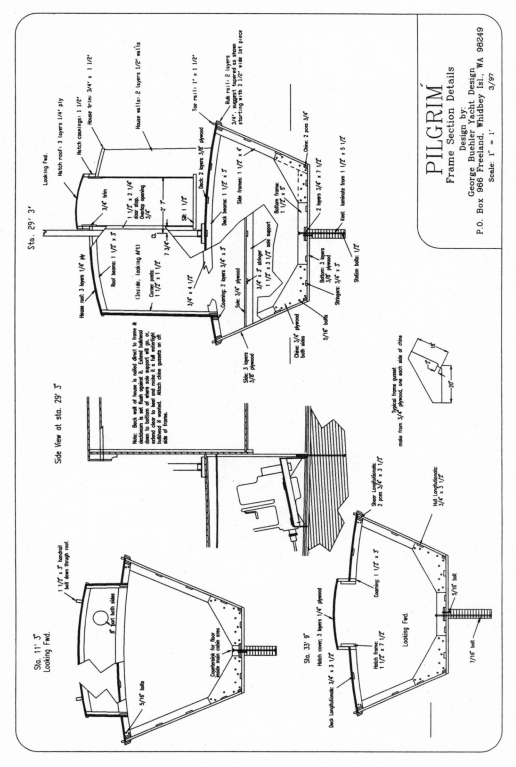

PILGRIM
Frame Section Details
Design by:
George Buehler Yacht Design
P.O. Box 966 Freeland, Whidbey Isl., WA 98249
Scale: 1" = 1'   3/97

Like the good dory she is, Pilgrim can handle the weight; as the figures in her hydrostatics show, the more she sinks, the more weight it takes to sink her, so if you don't mind living around a bunch of Jerry jugs for a week or two, you can carry another 75 gallons or so, giving you the range to easily hit Europe or Hawaii with reserve.

If I wanted to cruise like that, however, I'd go for a heavier boat like the 38-foot Duck. Of course I'm saying this from the perspective of a fat and complacent middle-aged guy with nothing to prove, but I remember when I was younger and unencumbered, and I had the time of my life in a sailboat that was 13 feet shorter, weighed less, and had accommodations even more Spartan than this boat. And I'll *never* forget those two years, either, let me tell you. So if you're a young punk doing some menial and boring job that you'd like to ditch and go cruising but you don't have any money, or if you're an old guy going through some sort of midlife crisis and don't have the time or energy (or, of course, money) to build a more substantial craft, or even if you're just a normal middle-class guy, maybe even a Captain of Industry, and just want a basic boat for a vacation retreat and no-hassle coastal cruising, Pilgrim will do it for you.

BACK AT THE BEGINNING of this book I talked about the cruising sailboats that were common up to the early 1970s: simple, stout, and reliable craft designed and built to cruise the oceans safely with minimal hassle. Because these boats were so simple and straightforward, they weren't all that expensive, and a young person or especially a working couple could build or buy one and have it paid for before they were too feeble to use it.

The Troller Yacht concept follows exactly the same approach: simple, stout, and reliable powerboats designed to cruise the oceans safely with minimal hassle. You won't see much about these kinds of boats in today's advertiser-driven marine press, and many of the folks at the yacht club bar won't understand what they're about, so you'll have to decide for yourself whether or not you agree with the concept behind these boats. To me, the simplicity, safety, and reliability of the Troller Yachts and their low-tech sailing cousins make a great deal of sense for a long-range ocean cruiser, whether you can afford to spend three times more for a same-size boat or not.

Well, I appreciate your patience in reading through all this and I hope you found it interesting. As they say in Ballard (the Scandahoovian part of Seattle): "Yah vell, and that's what I think about *that!*"

When loaded down with two people and gear, the canoe weighs (displaces) 400 pounds. The log pond boat weighs 3,000 pounds. With both boats being the same length, there must be a tremendous difference in hull shape to account for the radically different displacements. I could describe this difference by saying, "That canoe boat, there isn't much to her. She's skinny as a fence rail, draws so little water she'll float on a heavy dew, and has so little freeboard you can touch the water almost by looking at it. Mine's built of 1/4-inch glued cedar strips, but Jim Bob down the swamp's got one just the same only made of aluminum no thicker'n a Budweiser can. She ain't much, but she moves through the water so easily even I don't mind paddling her." That description is accurate and forms a good picture of the shape of the boat's hull, but look how much easier it is just to say, "She has a D/L of 36." This says exactly the same thing. It tells us that the hull has an extremely light displacement; because she weighs so little, she obviously must be built very lightly—or to translate that into boat-speak, she has very thin scantlings.

Here's how I'd have to describe the log pond push boat without referring to its D/L ratio: "She's half as wide as she is long, and needs 3 feet of water to float. She's built of 3/16-inch steel plate with closely spaced 1/4- × 1-inch longitudinals. She has a 100-horsepower Merc in a well with a full cage around the prop, and can push and pull the biggest logs without a strain." If you've never heard of a log pond push boat (used to shuttle floating logs stored around sawmills), you can probably picture one from this. But as descriptive as this is, it's much easier and more accurate to say, "My 16-foot boom boat has a D/L of 272." That tells us the boat is very heavy displacement, and as a result has a heavily built hull.

Technical descriptions may provide accurate information, but they sure lack color, unless you really know the subject. Then your imagination can kick in and you can see things as clearly as the poetry inside you allows. Thus, two guys in The Old Naval Architects Home can sit at a table and one can say, "Sven's first boat, old *Ingaborg*, was 41 feet long and had a D/L of 190. That new one he got, that *Dauntless*, she's 43 feet long and has a D/L of 347," and they could sit and chew their snoose and sip their drinks and visualize clearly that the *Ingaborg* had an old-time, easily driven troller type of hull, and *Dauntless* was a modern work platform with a huge engine to power her through whatever the ocean serves up, able to pack four times the fish of *Ingaborg* while costing 10 times more to buy and four times more to operate, which was why, when the fishing turned sour, Sven could no longer make the payments on his boat and ended up washing dishes down at the Sons of Norway.

DWL (Drawn Waterline) is the line where the designer hopes the boat will float—the waterline you see on the plans, and the point from which the designer made all the calculations for displacement, weight, stability, or other guesses. Remember, just because the designer calls it the waterline doesn't mean the boat will float there. To do that, the boat needs to weigh the same as its calculated displacement. In practice, we want our voyaging boat to float a few inches high at the launch, so when we're ready to cruise and load it down with personal effects, provisions, and fuel, she'll sit on her DWL (loaded for a major voyage, she'll start a little below her marks). This being the case, a more accurate term for DWL is *Load Waterline* (LWL), because the waterline on the plan is almost always meant to show the boat in cruising trim.

There's a story about a prominent local boat designer who had the funds to do what many secretly dream of doing. On launching day for one of his designs, he arranged to meet the crane operator at sunup. The boat was lowered into the water, the designer waded around it and marked the actual floating waterline, then the boat was lifted back out and the waterline painted on. At the launching ceremonies later, the crowd was extremely impressed when the boat floated right on her marks! Very few actually do.

Hull Speed is the maximum velocity at which a boat can travel *through* the water (not slide over the top of the water; see *Planing Hulls*). A boat's maximum hull speed is equal to 1.34 times the square root of its waterline length. If you try to drive a displacement hull faster than that, the boat starts sinking.

Around the turn of the century, sailing yachts were rated by their LWL, not LOA, and to get a competitive edge when racing against boats in the same class, the hulls kept getting longer on deck while the waterline length stayed the same. That's why you'd see racing boats like Herreshoff's Bar Harbor 30, which was 30 feet on the waterline but 50 feet on deck. When these boats heeled, their waterlines would lengthen and so the boats went faster.

You might remember old-time sailing yarns about a crazy captain, pistols in both hands, standing on the quarterdeck and yelling that he'd shoot the man who eases sail, as the ship, burdened down by acres of canvas, careens along in a gale then suddenly dives down through a sea and disappears with all hands. Kipling wrote a great description of this in *Captains Courageous*, and I'm sure it happened more than once in real life. I've almost done it myself with a sailboat. A gust hit me as I was roaring along downwind off California, and the boat started sinking, looking for more waterline to support the extra horsepower from the heavy wind gust. All hatches and portlites were closed, so I was more likely to lose the rig or get washed out of the cockpit than sink, but water was even with the deck before I got her reefed down.

LOA (Length Overall) means the entire boat, from the tip of its bow stem, bowsprit, pulpit, or anchor housing to the very last bit of hull in back. Technically, outboard rudders are included, too.

LOD (Length on Deck) is the boat measured on the deck less any bolt-ons like sprits or rudders.

LWL (Length on Waterline) is the hull's length in the water. The proper description of a boat's length depends on where you are: In the cocktail lounge it's LOA; in the harbormaster's office it's LOD; to the tax assessor it's LWL.

Planing Hulls are designed to raise up and scoot across the top of the water. To do this they need to have flat sections aft and be very lightweight. Although there are plenty of planing-type cabin cruisers on the water—some of them really spectacular—they don't have enough volume either to carry all a voyager's gear or the fuel needed to go very far. Recently I read about a 60-footer that can go from Florida to the Bahamas faster than it takes to clear customs in Freeport and head for the fuel dock to juice up its twin 1,000-horsepower turbocharged diesels.

V/L	Speed (knots)	Horsepower Required
1.5	9.8	144
2.0	13.1	292
2.5	16.4	424
3.0	19.7	565

Semiplaning hulls are designed to travel faster than hull speed without actually climbing completely up on top of the water. Compared with planing hulls, semiplaning boats are built more heavily and sit deeper in the water, and so have extra displacement to pack more weight. Semiplaning hulls are quite common; many so-called "trawler yachts" are actually semiplaning hulls. That extra speed potential comes at a cost, however. For example, let's take the fine-lined displacement design, 39,000-pounds displacement, 43 feet on the waterline, flatten the midsection, and add a broad transom with the beam carried all the way aft; this is the hull form necessary for brute power to start forcing the boat out of the water rather than into it.

Prismatic Coefficient, like *block coefficient,* is based on a block, but this time the block has the same cross-section area as the hull does at its largest (normally about midships) station. "Normal" is between 0.52 and 0.64; the prismatic coefficient is supposed to show if the boat's ends are fat or narrow.

V/L (Speed to Length Ratio) refers to the boat's actual speed ("velocity," for the engineering inclined) expressed as a percentage of its hull speed.

Auxiliary Sail

THE ACCOMPANYING ILLUSTRATION shows the spars, rigging, and sails for the 48-foot Alcina; you can use this as a guide if you want to add a similar system to your boat. Unlike the fussy, overdesigned rigs that power modern sailboats, a cruising powerboat's auxiliary sail plan can be designed almost by ear—after all, these boats derive not from a racing sailboat heritage but from simple, everyday workboats. We don't care about squeezing out a half-knot of upwind speed. We want a multipurpose rig that will reduce rolling underway and at anchor, can lift aboard heavy cargo, and will get us home should the engine quit. For that you don't need rocket science, just rugged simplicity.

The mast is used both to support the sail rig and to hoist aboard heavy things such as a skiff, a motorcycle, a drum of fuel, or the like. Your cargo-hoisting needs are a more important factor than the sail plan in determining mast location, because the sails are for off-wind use and just about any broad shape will work; but it all depends on how your boat is configured. I prefer the design shown here, with its central wheelhouse with flush aft deck, because it provides the best deck storage and the best interior arrangement for long-term living aboard. You'd step the mast immediately aft of a central wheelhouse; this positions the boom directly over the best storage spot for a skiff and other heavy things, and it moves the mainsail way aft so that it acts as a riding sail, making it easy to heave-to at sea or at anchor.

With an aft-mounted wheelhouse you'll be storing deck cargo forward, and the mast will have to go forward of the wheelhouse. This means you'll have to figure out a way to get some sail far enough aft to hold the nose up into the wind for anchoring or riding. You could sheet the sail to the back of the wheelhouse, although you'd have to mount any antennas aft of that or lower them when you wanted to swing the boom outboard. You could also use a boomless sail sheeted to the back of the house, with a cargo boom mounted on the front of the mast for hoisting things aboard.

With either rig, the mast is stepped on deck, preferably on top of a heavy bulkhead. If that isn't possible, you'll need a heavy mast step spanning two deck beams, stout enough to take the heavy load. You'll need a truly heavy-duty mast; you'll use it regularly to hoist aboard heavy loads, and if you run aground someday, you could use a tackle atop the mast to pull the boat onto its beam ends, reducing draft while you winch or tow it off.

A typical aluminum sailboat spar won't handle this kind of load. I'd make the mast from wood, either from an evergreen tree of appropriate size or laminated from 2-by material. I like the look of oiled wood, not to mention its feel and the sound of rope hitting it. But steel pipe will work fine as well, although it lacks the aesthetic angle. It's practical, though; some people even run their dry exhaust up a pipe mast, making it a kind of superstack.

An aft-mounted mast is supported by a bracket attached to the back of the house along with wire stays: two shrouds per side and a forestay running to the stem; I'd use 3/8-inch-diameter 6 × 7 weave galvanized wire. The stays need to be securely attached to the hull. With a steel hull you can weld attachment points to the edge of the deck, but a wood or glass hull will need actual chainplates bolted to the side of the hull. I'd use 5/16- or 3/8-inch-thick by 3-inch-wide straps, 18 to 24 inches long, mounted to the outside of the hull and bent to go over the rubrail and rail cap. Extend them 2 inches above the rail or sheer so there's room to attach the turnbuckles, which should be galvanized, 5/8 inch or bigger.

If you keep the boat near a low bridge or if you think you might want to explore a canal system or the inland waterways someday, you can make the mast stowable by installing a tabernacle (a big hinge) at a point higher than the wheelhouse. This system looks fragile but it isn't; Dutch canal boats have used these rigs for centuries. To lower the mast you'd pull the pin in the tabernacle, loosen the sidestays, and fold the mast down facing forward.

The boom supports the riding sail and also hoists aboard our skiff and motorcycle and so needs to be heavy enough to take a good load.

A friend of mine once even used his to hoist an engine out of a neighbor's sailboat. Like the mast, the boom can be of solid wood or pipe. Again, I like wood, and I'd use a heavy piece of fir, like a 4 × 6, attached to the mast with a typical gooseneck welded up from mild steel. You could even use wood jaws, just like a Grand Banks schooner.

You'll need an attachment point on the boom's top outer end to hook the two- or three-part tackle that serves as both a topping lift when running under sail and as a way to raise and lower the boom when using it as a cargo hoist. The other end of this tackle runs through a block at the masthead, then down to a cleat on the mast. All lines should be at least 3/8-inch diameter, and 1/2-stuff is much easier to grip.

On the boom's bottom outer end you'll need an attachment point for a three- or four-part tackle used for lifting and lowering deck cargo. This tackle runs to a cleat on the boom back near the mast. Some people use small winches instead of tackles. Often these are electric winches, although when these quit—and being electric they will if they're around salt water long enough—they'll leave you in the lurch. A better system uses a sailboat-style winch mounted on the boom, and the best system uses a large manual boat-trailer winch with a self-storing cable.

The sails need to be rugged, especially the main, or riding sail, which should be made from heavy Dacron, cut flat with no shape, and with a line of reefing points positioned to cut the sail's size almost in half. You can attach the riding sail to the mast and boom with slides running on sail track, or you can lace it on loosely using 5/16- or 3/8-inch line. Sail track is simpler because it's easier to remove the sail. You'd hoist the sail using a line running through a block at the masthead, then back down to a cleat on the mast or to a pinrail mounted to the shrouds. Since sunlight kills Dacron, you'll need a sail cover when you're anchored (and a place to store the sail cover when you're not).

The headsail needs to be heavy, too, but it shouldn't be cut flat, as normally it will be used for sailing off-wind. The headsail is attached to the headstay with piston-style hanks and sheeted down to the deck. I'd just use one sheet: you'll never be short-tacking up a narrow channel with this sail; it's only hoisted at sea, and in the long run it's easier to walk the sheet to the other side when you change course rather than continually tripping over a loose sheet flopping around on the other side of the boat.

You'll need to see underneath the headsail when you're driving, so the luff should be cut at least 4 feet shorter than the length of the headstay, with the tack attached to the stem fitting by a line at least 2 and preferably 3 feet long. The sail is hoisted by a line running through a block at the masthead and down to a cleat or a pinrail. If you're in port or just making day trips, you can remove the sail from the stay, but when cruising keep it hanked on and stuffed in a sail bag tied off to the pulpit if you have one, or the stay itself if you don't.

A roller-furling headsail sounds good on the surface, but this system adds considerable windage as well as at least $1,500 (for a 40-footer) to the boat's price. And it's just one more system to maintain and have fail when you need it most, so I don't recommend one.

Above all, this sail plan is rugged and simple. Don't get carried away! This isn't a sailboat and we don't need a sailboat's systems; we want a sail *assist* system. So when you're shopping for rigging items, just walk right on past the sailboat stuff at the marine toy store.

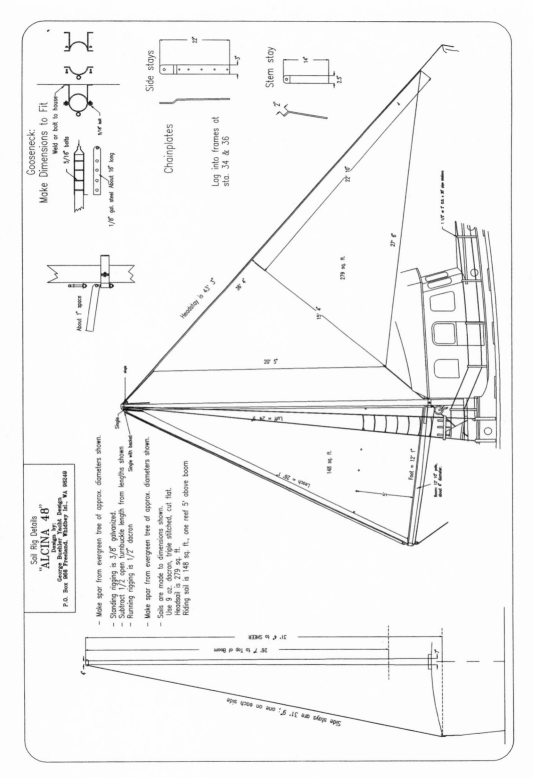

Sail Rig Details
"ALCINA 48"
Design by:
George Buehler Yacht Design
P.O. Box 966 Freeland, Whidbey Isl., WA 98249

- Make spar from evergreen tree of approx. diameters shown.

- Standing rigging is 3/8" galvanized.
- Subtract 1/2 open turnbuckle length from lengths shown
- Running rigging is 1/2" dacron

- Make spar from evergreen tree of approx. diameters shown.

- Sails are made to dimensions shown.
  Use 9 oz. dacron, triple stitched, cut flat.
  Headsail is 279 sq. ft.
  Riding sail is 148 sq. ft., one reef 5' above boom

Gooseneck:
Make Dimensions to Fit

Weld or bolt to house

5/16" bolts

5/16" bolt

1/8" gal. steel About 16" long

About 1" space

Side stays

22"

5"

Stem stay

14"

2.5"

Chainplates

2"

Log into frames at
sta. 34 & 36

Single

Single

Single with becket

Headstay is 43' 3"

36' 4"

22' 10"

15' 4"

27' 6"

279 sq. ft.

20' 5"

Luff = 24' 9"

148 sq. ft.

Leach = 26' 1"

Foot = 12' 1"

Boom: 12' 10" pole,
about 4" diameter.

1 1/2" or 2" O.D. x 36' pipe mizzen

31' 4" to SHEER

26' 7" to Top of Boom

Side stays are 31' 9"; one on each side

Suggested Reading

THROUGHOUT THIS BOOK I've mentioned other books I thought might be helpful in understanding a particular subject. Here's a more extensive list of books I like and use for reference. Some are out of print, but they do show up in secondhand bookstores.

DESIGN

THE *COMMON SENSE OF YACHT DESIGN* by L. Francis Herreshoff (Caravan Maritime Books), and *Yacht Designing and Planning* by Howard Chapelle (W. W. Norton), are excellent reference books written by two guys who really knew their stuff. Herreshoff is fun to read—a lifelong bachelor, rather prissy about many things, and even wordier than me. His books are full of memorable quotes, several of which I've mentioned in this book. If you're interested in designing your own boat, read these guys, but then see if you can find *Designing Small Boats for Fun and Profit*, by V. B. Crockett. Published in 1953 by D. Van Nostrand, this book does for boat design what *Volkswagen Repair for the Complete Idiot* did for car repair and *Buehler's Backyard Boatbuilding* (if you'll forgive me) does for wood boatbuilding. I've always wondered why somebody like *WoodenBoat* doesn't bring Crockett's book back.

BUILDING

HOWARD CHAPELLE'S *BOATBUILDING* (W. W. Norton) is known as the wood boatbuilder's Bible and is a wonderful reference work. *Buehler's Backyard Boatbuilding,* by me, published by International Marine and edited by the same pain in the neck who helped me with this book, tells how to build large wood and plywood boats from an amateur's point of view. I wrote it because I thought there was a need for a book that talks about all the stuff the pros like Chapelle don't mention.

Ferro-Cement: Design, Techniques, and Application, by Bruce Bingham (Cornell Maritime Press), is an excellent building book. I've discussed the downside of cement boats, but there is nothing wrong with the material when it's used right, and there are times when it makes sense. I wish I could recommend a steel or aluminum building book, but so far the ones I've seen are hard to follow if you don't already know what you're doing. Publishers: There's a market out there for a steel backyard boatbuilding book! However, *Steel Away,* by LeCain Smith and Sheila Moir (Windrose Productions), is a good general reference about metal boats, although the way they dismiss chine hulls seems to show a basic ignorance; but then these guys aren't builders or designers and aren't writing from that perspective. The book does a good job of detailing all the special things about dealing with metal: installing through-hulls, protecting from corrosion, and so on. It also lists many steel builders and designers, both in the United States and around the world.

Practical Yacht Joinery, by Fred Bingham (International Marine), shows how boat interiors are made. *Build the New Instant Boats,* by Dynamite Payson (International Marine), is handy if you're interested in building your own skiff. *Designer's Notebook,* by Ian Nicolson, now out of print, is full of ideas about installing or building stuff to make a boat more comfortable or convenient. I wish I had written it. Or perhaps it's more accurate to say I wish I knew all that stuff and had been *able* to write it.

MAINTENANCE

MARINE DIESEL ENGINES, by Nigel Calder, and *12-Volt Bible,* by Minor Brotherton (both from International Marine), are good reference books. One of the best, believe it or not, is *Maintenance,* from the Time-Life Books boating series. This book goes into wonderful detail using absolutely clear illustrations about how to do all sorts of stuff, from fixing a hole in a plastic boat to changing the points in a gas engine. It even has a big section on how to fix a damaged ferrocement boat! It's one of the best how-to books I've ever seen.

GENERAL INFORMATION

ROBERT BEEBE'S *VOYAGING UNDER POWER* (International Marine) was the only book about long-range powerboat cruising out there until this one. It's well worth reading, both in its original and revised edition. The classic *Cruising Under Sail,* by Eric and Susan Hiscock (International Marine), should be owned by everyone cruising any kind of boat. Eric and Susan Hiscock were world cruisers who wrote the first real how-to books on the subject. In 1981, a new edition of this book came out that combined two previous guides, *Cruising Under Sail* and *Voyaging Under Sail.* The best thing about this book is that it's written from the perspective of people with "normal" incomes who take things easy. For instance, their first boat didn't have an engine, but their next boat, a 30-footer, had a small inboard with a 5-gallon tank. Hiscock wrote that he decided he wanted more fuel to be able to power through some of the horse latitudes (where wind is scarce), so they carried an extra 3 gallons. Their last boat was a heavy steel 45-footer, which ended up being too much for them to handle comfortably. I always wondered why they didn't just switch to power, but then, they were British, which says it all.

Song of the Sirens, by Ernest Gann, is out of print but you can find it in used-book stores. Gann was a boat-crazy airline pilot as well as a very successful writer and novelist. This book combines his experiences as a West Coast commercial fisherman with some of his sailing adventures. And while I'm recommending books, you might want to read Gann's *Fate Is the Hunter,* which details his experiences as one of the early airline captains. I remember him writing about being a young copilot in a DC 2, lost in the fog and expecting to die any second, and hearing the captain say, "I told Wilbur, I told Orville, I told Glenn Curtis, I told all them fellas these damned things would never work."

Index

Page numbers in **bold** refer to illustrations.

engine, diesel manufacturers:
  Caterpillar, 45; Cummins, 45, 46,
  50; Detroit Diesel, **45**, 47; Deutz
  (German), 47; Ford, 45, 46; Gardner
  (British), 47-48; GM/Bedford diesels,
  47; Hundesteds (Denmark), 48; Jimmy
  Diesels, 47; John Deere/Lugger, 45,
  46; Lister (British), 48; Sabb
  (Norwegian), 48, 50, 51
exhaust system, 105-106

F

Farmer, Weston, 129
ferrocement hull construction, 83-85
fiberglass hull construction, 81-82
flopper-stoppers, 40
foot-pound, 49
Ford engine, 45, 46
Frances, (troller), 24, **102,**, 144
fuel system/fuel tanks, 93-96:
  cleanliness, 39; flow meter, 94-95;
  lines, 95; tank layout, **92**, 94

G

galley *See* kitchen
Garden, William, 114
Gardner (British) engine, 47-48
generators (gensets), 90-91
Geo Shima, 13
Gilmer, Thomas, 116
GM/Bedford diesel engines, 47
Goudy & Stevens, 70
Gulf Coast shrimpers, 117

H

Half-Safe, 22
halibut schooners, 13, **14**, 40
Halverson, Boyer, 33
Hammond, Fred, **70, 71**, 122-125
Hand, William, 116
handholds, 68
heater units, 101, 101-102
Herreshoff, L. Francis, 25, 102, 114
Herreshoff, Nathanael, 129
Hiscock, Eric and Susan, 12, 17, 18
horsepower, 49-53: continuous-duty, 49;
  efficient use of, 51; propeller-shaft,
  51; torque, 50

hull: bulbous bow, 59-60; cold-moulded
  construction, 121-125; efficiency, 24;
  hydrostatic calculations, **57**; round
  bottom, 59; sail/commercial
  conversion, 115-119; seakindly, 58-60;
  seaworthiness, 55-58; single-chine, 59
  stability, 58; symmetry, 60-61
Hundesteds (Denmark) engine, 48
hydraulic: anchor winch, 102-103, **102,
  103**; stabilizers, 40-41; steering,
  96, 97-98
hydrostatic calculations: hull forms, **57**

I

Icelandic trawler, 14-15, **15**
ignition systems, 44
Ingrid, 26-27
inverter, 90

J

Jimmy Diesels, 47
John Deere/Lugger, 45, 46
joule, 49

K

keel, 62
keel cooler, **108**
kitchen, 32, 67: refrigeration, 100-101;
  stove fuel, 99-100

L

Leishman, James, 21, 22
Lifeboat Ketch 44 (double-ender), 114
lights, cabin, 101
Lister (British), 48, 51
lofting, 134-135
Luke, Paul, 70

M

Marchaj, C. A., 56
Marco Polo 55 (motorsailer), 115
Millereck, Don, 147
Millereck, Jeff, 147
Mister Coffee, 50
Motorboating & Sailing, 115

N

naval architect, 128
New England sardine carrier, **116**, 118
newton, 49
noise, 110-111
Nordhavens (trawler yacht), 23